IMAGES
of England

HOLBORN, BLOOMSBURY AND CLERKENWELL

Tottenham Court Road from St Giles Circus, *c.* 1920. A busy scene at Holborn's western extremity. The street was overlooked by the flamboyant YMCA building (1911) whose style was in marked contrast to the concrete brutality of its successor of 1971. The older building on the Great Russell Street corner was more typical of the sort of properties with which Tottenham Court Road became lined as the formerly rural road became built up from the mid-eighteenth century. One of London's earliest bus stops may be seen, centre left. This was made of wood and was the property of the London General Omnibus Company, forerunners of London Transport.

IMAGES
of England

HOLBORN, BLOOMSBURY
AND CLERKENWELL

Compiled by
Brian Girling

TEMPUS

First published 1999
Copyright © Brian Girling, 1999

Tempus Publishing Limited
The Mill, Brimscombe Port,
Stroud, Gloucestershire, GL5 2QG

ISBN 0 7524 1539 5

Typesetting and origination by
Tempus Publishing Limited
Printed in Great Britain by
Midway Clark Printing, Wiltshire

Judd Street, Bloomsbury, 21 July 1907. Part of the vast crowd of onlookers (mostly cloth-capped youths) who turned out to view the spectacle of a fire at the Midland Furnishing Company's premises in Judd Street (see pp. 86 and 87). There was a considerable police presence to control the crowds and to clear a path for the firefighters with their horse-drawn appliances. The background shows some of Judd Street's original houses (since demolished), together with a popular local shop, a branch of Walton, Hassell & Port, the grocers. There was a touch of Regency elegance next door at No. 54, with a stucco front and some fancy ironwork around the balcony. Clare Court, a smart block of flats from the 1930s, stands here now.

Contents

Acknowledgements

For their pictorial contributions to this book, I would like to thank Camden Local Studies and Archives Centre; Judge's Postcards, Hastings; and David Brewster. For their unfailing helpfulness at all times, my special thanks go to the staff at Camden Local Studies and Archives Centre and, as ever, there is a big thank you to transport historians R.W. Kidner and David Brewster for their help and guidance. The facilities of the Westminster Archives Centre and Guildhall Library have once again proved invaluable. Books consulted include: *Streets of Bloomsbury & Fitzrovia*, Camden History Society; *East of Bloomsbury*, David A. Hayes, Camden History Society; *Bloomsbury, Fitzrovia and Soho* and *Fleet Street, Holborn and the Inns of Court*, both by Roger Hudson; *Bloomsbury Past*, Richard Tames; *An Historical Walk Through Clerkenwell*, Mary Cosh; *Historic Clerkenwell*, London City Walk; *London Underground Stations*, David Leboff; *The London Encyclopaedia*, Ben Weinreb and Christopher Hibbert; *The Buildings of England – London, vol. 4*, Bridget Cherry and Nikolaus Pevsner; *The Cinemas of Camden*, Mark Aston; *Islington*, David Withey and Vada Hart; *Living London*, George R. Sims.

Kirby Street, Holborn, *c.* 1911. A militant demonstration, possibly during the great London strike of 1911, in this street of commercial properties which links Cross Street with Greville Street (then called Charles Street). Kirby Street was named after Bishop Kirby of Ely, who in the thirteenth century built Ely House, the London palace of the Bishops of Ely.

Introduction

This book takes a nostalgic look at a fascinating multi-faceted slice of central London which lies along parts of the boundaries of the Cities of London and Westminster, and takes in areas of the former Metropolitan Boroughs of Holborn, St Pancras, Finsbury and Islington, now the London Boroughs of Camden and Islington.

The tour begins at ancient St Giles, where London's Great Plague began in late 1664 and where the nightmarish squalor of Seven Dials inspired Hogarth in the eighteenth century. It then follows the Roman road to the City of London and the 'Hole Bourne', a reach of the River Fleet which gave its name to a parish and a borough. Along the way is a stop at an ancient inn with a tale of high treason, and at a fire-wrecked chemist's warehouse with a history. There is also a look at part of Legal London, a rarefied world where the sequestered gas-lit quadrangles of Lincoln's Inn and Gray's Inn still give a taste of a London which otherwise vanished long ago.

A look at London's first new roads of the twentieth century, Kingsway and Aldwych, built in place of the tottering tenements of Clare Market and Old Drury Lane, leads northwards to the cool, elegant terraces of Bloomsbury, where in the early 1900s the literati of the Bloomsbury Group were a cultural elite alongside grand (and less grand) hotels and the universities of London's most concentrated academic quarter. Here, too, is Medical London with its renowned hospitals, and Children's London with the Hospital for Sick Children and the playgrounds of Coram's Fields where no adult may enter unless a child will take them in.

Further north again, the densely populated northern parts of Bloomsbury are studied, with their old streets and houses before they were replaced by the bright modern flats of post-war London, and where the populace was entertained by the diversions offered by the Euston Music Hall. There is also a look at Tottenham Court Road with its long tradition of furniture retailing, where Bloomsbury merges into Fitzrovia and where one of London's best known places of entertainment arose on the site of a brewery.

The final chapter explores the City of London's first suburb, Clerkenwell, where from the twelfth century great monastic foundations flourished until they were dissolved by Henry VIII. This is also where a few craftsmen displaced by the Great Fire of London in 1666 settled, beginning a continuing tradition of occupancy by jewellers, clock-makers and similar specialists.

The tour moves on to Clerkenwell's hillier northern reaches, where the discovery in the seventeenth century of the health-giving properties of the area's natural springs and wells spawned numerous spas and pleasure resorts. The name of one of them, Sadler's Wells, is famed worldwide, but not for its original reason – the music came later.

There is a long look at the streets of Clerkenwell, ranging from the colourful crowded byways of the Italian quarter to the late Victorian Rosebery Avenue with its viaduct and smart electric trams. Then the tour goes onward to the hilly heights where the Lloyd-Bakers built their estate of almost Grecian-style houses and where the New River Company laid out a spacious townscape of broad streets and plain terraces.

The final pages follow King's Cross Road as it meanders along the course of the now underground River Fleet, the unseen stream which, with its tributaries, is close to many of the scenes shown on the following pages.

Most of the photographs are appearing in print here for the first time and reproductions of many of them may be obtained from Brian Girling, 17 Devonshire Road, Harrow, HA1 4LS.

Opulence in Bloomsbury: Hotel Russell, Russell Square, *c.* 1920. The towering terracotta and rich red brickwork of Hotel Russell's late Victorian design rises high above the plain brick terraces of an earlier Bloomsbury. The hotel was the work of architect C. Fitzroy Doll whose neighbouring but now sadly departed Imperial Hotel was an even more elaborate affair (see p. 68). Part of Woburn Place is in the distance, as yet unwidened and still with its original Georgian houses. The tower of St Pancras New Church makes an appearance on the horizon.

One

Holborn

High Holborn from Kingsway, *c.* 1919. Holborn is unique among London's former metropolitan boroughs in that its name is also that of its principal thoroughfare. It is actually 'High Holborn' for much of its length, but Londoners habitually refer to it all as 'Holborn'. The street itself is on the line of a road built by the Romans as a route from the New Gate in the city wall of Londinium (London) towards the west of England. By the thirteenth century it was a busy commercial road known as 'Holeburnstreete', serving the City of London, which lay beyond the steep-sided valley of the Hole Bourne, or River Fleet. It was not until Victorian times that the valley was bridged by one of the engineering triumphs of that era, Holborn Viaduct. The western end of what is now High Holborn was called Broad Street until the 1930s. The photograph catches High Holborn as its modest eighteenth- and nineteenth-century buildings were being replaced by the grander structures of the twentieth century. Dominating everything was the still partly built Pearl Assurance building which was begun in 1912 and would take many more years to complete. An extension to the Pearl building swallowed up the site of the Holborn Empire, a popular theatre where Albert Chevalier and Dan Leno once performed. To the right is Holborn Underground station which was built on the Kingsway corner for the Great Northern, Piccadilly and Brompton Railway Company. The station opened on 15 December 1906 and featured the distinctive blood-red tiles of the early Piccadilly Tube stations. The station was given its present Portland stone finish in 1930 and was additionally served by Central Line trains from 25 September 1933 following the closure of nearby British Museum station.

Charing Cross Road by New Oxford Street, *c.* 1911. The days of these Victorian-style horse buses were numbered with the latest motor omnibuses poised to drive the last of them off London's roads. The backdrop of shops topped by Imperial Mansions would prove more resilient, but in the 1960s their site would be transformed by the arrival of the towering thirty-five-storey Centre Point with its attendant ground level water features and modern road layout. Charing Cross Road was a creation of the 1880s, its New Oxford Street end a widening of old Crown Street, St Giles. It would later achieve fame for its bookshops and theatres with the music trade establishing London's 'Tin Pan Alley' in nearby Denmark Street.

Shaftesbury Avenue with High Street, St Giles and Broad Street (High Holborn), *c.* 1910. Westminster's section of the new Shaftesbury Avenue cut through Soho's slums in the 1880s but the Holborn part (east of Cambridge Circus) incorporated much of pre-existing Dudley Street (left) and part of Broad Street, one of whose old terraces is seen on the right. This still survives. The buildings facing the camera were part of High Street, St Giles, which was once the principal street of a rural village. St Giles Court was built here for the Ministry of Supply in 1950.

St Giles High Street, c. 1936. This is a 1930s image of a street whose long history has taken it from a muddy village high street to a modern urban thoroughfare, although its narrowness is still a reminder of former times. Old St Giles was a famously squalid place – London's Great Plague broke out here late in 1664 – and by Victorian times the St Giles rookery had become one of the capital's more notorious slums. The Victorians swept it all away and in an attempt at respectability renamed the road High Street, Bloomsbury (which can still be seen on an old frontage), but the former name prevailed. In the 1930s, London's profusion of High Street names were prefixed with their localities and St Giles High Street was born. Numbers 3 to 11 are shown here, leading to Clarkes Mews further along. St Giles Court is here now. (Camden Local Studies and Archives Centre)

St Giles-in-the-Fields, High Street, c. 1912. The history of the church can be traced back to 1101 when Matilda, wife of Henry I, founded a leper hospital in the fields to the west of London. Following the closure of the hospital in 1539, its chapel became the parish church of the village which had grown up around it. A new church was built in 1630 and lasted until 1734 when the church we know today was built by Henry Flitcroft, whose name lives on in nearby Flitcroft Street.

Shaftesbury Avenue, 7 July 1903. Residents of St Giles, who like most Londoners enjoyed a free show, turned out to cheer President Loubet of France whose carriage procession passed along Shaftesbury Avenue during one of his visits to this country. Britain's friendly relationship with France in Edwardian times, aided by President Loubet's visits, led in 1904 to the establishment of the *Entente Cordiale* between the two nations. The background shows the shop of James Rutherford, clothes dealer, whose premises were originally part of Dudley Street before that road was absorbed into the new Shaftesbury Avenue in the 1880s.

Shaftesbury Avenue, c. 1918. Two doors from James Rutherford's shop was Antonio Agosti's Café des Sports, the Avenue Restaurant, where these charming ladies were on hand to welcome the diners. With its French-speaking staff, the restaurant was popular with visitors to the French Hospital which stood opposite. The hospital was built in French Renaissance style in 1899 but the building is now empty.

Seven Dials, c. 1896. Development of Seven Dials, a tiny circus from which seven streets radiated, began in the 1690s, a time when London was expanding westwards over the fields of St Giles. Like St Giles, Seven Dials became grossly over populated as its early ambitions of being a fashionable residential area became overwhelmed by crime, vice and poverty. The area was still far from salubrious in 1896 when this scene was photographed from Little St Andrew's Street towards Great St Andrew's Street (both now Monmouth Street), with Shorts Gardens centre right. The Crown pub, dated 1833, still stands. In more recent years, Seven Dials has become fashionable at last with its smart shops, pavement cafés and a stone pillar topped by a multi-faced sundial. This is a replica of the original which stood from 1694 to 1773 and was unveiled by Queen Beatrix of the Netherlands on 29 June 1989.

The Shaftesbury Hotel, Seven Dials, c. 1910. Edwardian gloom is evident in what was still an unfashionable quarter, with the Victorian Shaftesbury Hotel (now the Mountbatten) rising above soot-blackened earlier terraces. The side streets have since been renamed, with Great St Andrew's Street (Monmouth Street) on the right and Great White Lion Street (Mercer Street) centre left. Little Earl Street (Earlham Street) is at the far left with Gottlieb Vollmer's bakery occupying No. 19.

13

Broad Street (High Holborn), Princes Circus, *c.* 1913. To the left, topped by what Pevsner called 'a jolly rotunda', is the New Princes Theatre which opened on 26 December 1911 with a performance of *The Three Musketeers*. A cavalcade of theatrical luminaries have appeared here through the decades and in the 1920s D'Oyly Carte's Gilbert and Sullivan operas were staged. Sarah Bernhardt made her final London appearance here in 1921. The building was renamed Shaftesbury Theatre in 1962. In the foreground, a fine assembly of street furniture included that now elusive amenity, the underground public loo. The tree on the right obscures the site upon which the popular Oasis swimming pool would be built in the 1960s. This was formerly the site of wash houses and baths provided in 1853 for the unfortunate inhabitants of the St Giles slums.

Sudbury Dairy Company, Broad Street (High Holborn), c. 1908. Eggs were 2d a dozen, a glass of new milk was 1d and one could have had a pot of tea with a roll and butter for 4d at the Broad Street branch of this Soho-based dairy which occupied the Drury Lane corner. A post-war office block in brutalist concrete stands here now.

High Holborn looking towards Broad Street from Kingsway and Southampton Row, c. 1908. London's new street, Kingsway, had opened in 1905 but on its corner with High Holborn was a survivor from an earlier time, the Holborn Restaurant (left), which dated from 1874. This opulent building stood in Kingsway's predecessor, Little Queen Street, and had during its history accommodated swimming baths, casino, dance hall, grand restaurants and a host of smaller dining rooms. It was replaced in 1957 by the uninspiring Aviation House which is now itself being rebuilt. Beyond the Holborn Restaurant and just out of sight in Broad Street (High Holborn) was St Giles (Holborn) library (1894) and Holborn Town Hall (1906-8).

High Holborn from Little Queen Street (Kingsway), *c.* 1898. The shops on the right, including that of Hope Bros, hosiers, curved round into Little Queen Street, a narrow byway which accommodated the usual London mixture of shops, pubs and commercial premises. It would soon be swept away with the creation of London's grand new street, Kingsway, and the building of Holborn Underground station on the corner. Today, High Holborn is lined with large commercial blocks but the photograph reveals the street in its earlier guise when it was made up of plain terraces and a mass of small shops. The side turning by the bus was the long since departed Kingsgate Street.

High Holborn from Kingsway, *c.* 1908. The twentieth century has seen the total transformation of this view with new buildings replacing the old. In 1912 the Pearl Assurance Company began building their monumental new headquarters on the site of the properties on the right. Beyond was the soon to be demolished Inns of Court Hotel which ran through to Lincoln's Inn Fields. Buildings on the left would become the site of a new road, Procter Street, and spanned by Procter House (1960-2). The dark Regency building with its pediment and columns was home until 1897 of Day & Martin's blacking factory. It was demolished in the 1930s.

Clearing the site for the Pearl Assurance building, *c.* 1911. At the centre of this busy scene was a box-like structure, all that remained of an old shop which was still trading as everything around it was being demolished. Beyond, High Holborn is seen from an unfamiliar angle with Dane Street, right and the premises of Joseph Kaye the locksmith all but hidden behind a monstrous 'K'. Edward Harlene, the hair restorers, displayed a similar penchant for giant lettering, but between them, Batsford's bookshop had a more restrained image.

The First Avenue Hotel, High Holborn, *c.* 1920. This was a popular 300-bedroom hotel built on the site of the ill-fated Dukes Theatre which lasted only from 1866 to 1880 when fire destroyed it. The theatre was also known as the Royal Holborn and the Theatre Royal, Holborn. The hotel was a considerable landmark among its lowlier neighbours and there was a fine porch flanked by some particularly exotic lanterns. Air raids wrecked the hotel on 8 September 1940 and it was replaced in 1949 by an office block, First Avenue House.

High Holborn looking west, *c.* 1898. The First Avenue Hotel towers above older shops and pubs which included Henekey's Old Wine House, right, an 1831 rebuilding of an earlier establishment. The premises have been rebuilt once more as the Cittie of Yorke, whose owners proudly proclaim that there has been a pub here since 1430.

High Holborn looking east near Chancery Lane, *c.* 1908. There was still room for a cab rank in the middle of this busy road, with various types on view including a hansom, a 'growler' (four wheeler) and a new motor cab. The distinctive gold and white shop-front of J. Lyons' tea shop, popular caterers over many decades, stands out on the right. Chancery Lane station is on the left and the horizon is graced by the Gothic outline of the Prudential Assurance building.

Chancery Lane station, High Holborn, by Fulwood Place, *c.* 1904. As the twentieth century dawned, the north side of High Holborn still had a decidedly old fashioned look about it, but the new century soon brought a taste of the future with the opening on 30 July 1900 of the first section of the Central London Railway. This deep-level Tube line with its clean, efficient, electrically driven trains was a revelation to Londoners who were more used to steam-powered railways and horse-drawn street transportation. The first section of the Central London Railway, (now the Central line) ran from Shepherds Bush to Bank in the City of London with a flat fare of 2d. Inevitably, Londoners soon styled the line 'the twopenny Tube'. Apart from Bank, which uniquely had no surface buildings, the Central stations were built in a modern design with golden terracotta frontages. Chancery Lane was a typical example and started life as a single-storey building which was designed to be built on later. We see it here in its original state before Chancery Lane Station Chambers were built above in matching terracotta. The adjoining pub, La Criadera, was a flamboyantly Edwardian rebuilding of an earlier establishment. By the 1930s, the station's popularity necessitated a more efficient passenger access and reconstruction work began in 1932. In June 1934, new station entrances by Gray's Inn Road opened with a subterranean booking hall and escalators to replace the old lifts. With these new arrangements in place, the old entrance became redundant and closed, but it can still be seen, with shops on the street frontage and paint obscuring the old terracotta.

The Holborn Pub, High Holborn, by Gray's Inn Road, *c.* 1903. Victoriana runs riot in High Holborn where an intricate candelabra-like street lamp competes with the Holborn, a smaller corner pub yet one with a cupola and spire which would not have disgraced a City of London church. The Express Dairy next door displays the gentility of the era with a ladies' tea-room on the second floor, although delicate Victorian and Edwardian nostrils may have been offended by aromas rising from the smoking room below. In Gray's Inn Road, a number of hairdressing emporia competed for business with a profusion of signs. War damage preceded the rebuilding of the corner in 1955 with the drab Bishops House.

Staple Inn, Holborn, *c.* 1898. London's most famous row of half-timbered buildings looked very different in Victorian times when plaster covered what was then an unfashionable style of architecture. The buildings, of which the façades are the only surviving part of the originals, were put up in the sixteenth century along the street frontage of Staple Inn, a legal Inn of Chancery from 1378 to 1884. The name Staple Inn is thought to have originated with woolmongers or staplers who were the first occupants of Staple Inn early in the fourteenth century.

Picturesque London, OLD HOUSES, STAPLE INN, SHOWING CLARKSON'S OPTICAL STORES, 338, HIGH HOLBORN, W.C. 1. Opposite Gray's Inn Road.

Shop advertisement, High Holborn, *c.* 1920. Restoration revealed the wood-framed beauty of Staple Inn, its picturesque aspect becoming popular with local advertisers and, more famously, on Old Holborn tobacco packets. The Staple Inn frontage actually runs along two streets – Holborn to the left and High Holborn, right, where Clarkson's shop appears. The City of London boundary is also here.

Holborn and the Prudential Assurance building, *c.* 1920. The street is dominated by the Gothic splendours of the Prudential Assurance building with its towers, turrets and gables all concocted from fierce red brick and matching terracotta to designs by Alfred Waterhouse. Building began in 1879 with a second phase from 1899 to 1906, on the site of Furnival's Inn, another legal Inn of Chancery which was founded in 1383 and dissolved in 1817. Charles Dickens lived in Furnival's Inn while working as a newspaper reporter during the 1830s.

Holborn from Holborn Circus, *c.* 1920. Two of London's great retailing emporia were once located at the City of London end of Holborn. Gamage's, centre right, was founded in 1878 when Arthur Gamage began trading at a single small shop which prospered and expanded into an impressive department store next to the Prudential building until closure in 1972. Thomas Wallis' drapers, on the left, was also of Victorian origin, but was destroyed during a spectacular wartime fire on the night of 16-17 April 1941. The Mirror newspaper group built their headquarters on the site but this has now been demolished. The statue of Prince Albert, consort to Queen Victoria, politely raises its hat to passers-by.

Holborn Viaduct from Farringdon Street, c. 1920. Holborn takes its name from the stream known as the Hole Bourne (the river that flows through the holes or hollows), an upstream section of the River Fleet which reaches the Thames at Blackfriars. The river is still there but was culverted in 1733, all that is visible now being the old river valley. Steeply graded roads into the valley were a considerable hazard for the busy City traffic until 6 November 1869 when Queen Victoria opened Holborn Viaduct. The viaduct runs from Holborn Circus to Newgate but its scale is difficult to appreciate with buildings having been constructed along its length. It is only at Farringdon Street and Shoe Lane where the sides of it, in the form of bridges, can be seen.

Holborn Viaduct, c. 1920. The new viaduct gave a level run across the Fleet valley, a great improvement upon the steep, slippery streets of old. Holborn Viaduct was built to the designs of William Heywood, surveyor to the City, and features four bronze statues representing Commerce, Agriculture, Science and Fine Art. Of the four corner buildings containing steps down to Farringdon Street, only those on the left remain.

St Andrew's, Holborn, and war ruins from Shoe Lane, Holborn Viaduct, *c.* 1945. The Second World War transformed the area between Charterhouse Street and Holborn Viaduct into a nightmare landscape of bombsites and left Holborn's ancient parish church, St Andrew's, a burnt out ruin. St Andrew's was founded in Saxon times, the original wooden church being replaced by a stone-built Norman building with further reconstruction in the fifteenth century when the tower was built. It survived the Great Fire of London in 1666 but was rebuilt by Wren between 1684 and 1690. Following post-war restoration, the church re-opened in 1960.

War ruins from Shoe Lane, *c.* 1945. The camera has swung round to reveal the ruinous state of Charterhouse Street, right, with bomb damage extending through Holborn Circus to the remains of the Thomas Wallis store, centre left. A Gamage's delivery van makes its way past the gated entrance to Ely Place, centre, where the partly thirteenth-century St Etheldreda's church still stands.

Hatton Garden from Holborn Circus, *c.* 1908. Famously the centre of London's diamond and jewellery trade, Hatton Garden was named after Elizabethan courtier and Lord Chancellor Sir Christopher Hatton, who took over part of Ely House, the London palace of the medieval Bishops of Ely. Here, Sir Christopher created Hatton House and lived there in some style with Elizabeth I a frequent visitor. The garden of the Bishop's Palace was a particularly beautiful one, but around 1680 houses were built on part of it, during which time Hatton Street (now Hatton Garden) was laid out. The new houses on what was then the edge of London enjoyed rural views towards the hilly slopes of Pentonville and for a time Hatton Street became a fashionable place to live. As London spread ever outwards, the fields disappeared and the area became more commercial in character, with the first of the jewellers, for which the locality became famous, arriving around 1830. This Edwardian view captures the busy nature of the place when most of the houses were in multiple occupation by jewellers, diamond brokers and their associated traders. The premises of James Hicks, 'philosophical instrument maker', are in the centre of the photograph with an informative display of meteorological instruments, including a barometer. Close by, an old gas lamp advertises the presence in a narrow alley, called Ely Court, of Ye Olde Mitre, still an exceedingly picturesque pub whose history dates from 1546 when the first Mitre was built by the Bishops of Ely for the Palace servants. Formerly the pub had the disconcerting habit of opening its bars at different times in accordance with London licensing hours and those of the Isle of Ely, Cambridgeshire, under whose jurisdiction it fell. Today, the view from Holborn Circus shows a remarkable contrast. Although the right-hand side is seemingly little changed, with its jewellery businesses and even the Mitre's street lamp still in place, the left side is strictly twentieth-century in appearance, with modern flats, shops and some welcome greenery in the now widened roadway. A further element of this former enclave of Cambridgeshire in London can still be seen in the shape of the former chapel of the Bishop of Ely's palace, now the Catholic church of St Etheldreda, which is in Ely Place behind the houses on the right.

The aftermath of the Cross Street/Hatton Garden fire, seen from 55 Hatton Garden, 27 June 1914. During the early hours of 27 June 1914, a fire broke out in the chemical works of manufacturing chemists Hopkins & Williams, whose premises lay behind Cross Street and Hatton Garden. Fuelled by inflammable chemicals, the fire quickly took hold and caused a series of small explosions which awoke local residents from their slumbers. As the fire increased in intensity, it broke through into an intermediate building, on the right, and swept into 48 Hatton Garden, off the picture to the right, where the Baccarat Crystal Glass Co. had their showrooms. That building soon became an inferno and the beautiful displays of crystal glass on show there were destroyed. Access to the seat of the fire was very constricted and firefighters had to tackle the blaze from the windows of adjoining buildings. After many hours of hard-fought action, the fire was prevented from spreading further, but a number of businesses had been wrecked and one of Holborn's historic buildings lay in ruins. Hopkins & William's chemical stores were housed in a building which had begun life in 1796 as one of the Swedenborgians' New Jerusalem churches, before being sold some years later for the use of London's Gaelic-speaking Scottish Highlanders, whose services were conducted in their native tongue. Scottish Presbyterians took over the building in 1818, calling it the Caledonian Chapel, before they moved away to the Gothic splendours of their new church in Bloomsbury's Regent Square (p. 84). The old Cross Street chapel was bought back by the Swedenborgians in March 1827 and once again it became the New Jerusalem church, with services which were for a time so popular that it was necessary to buy a ticket to attend. The final service took place on 31 March 1872 and the property was then sold to the chemists who occupied it until its destruction. The chapel had narrowly avoided destruction by fires in the 1820s and again in 1912 when a block of buildings at the corner of Cross Street and Great Saffron Hill was burnt down. These rebuilt premises can be seen beyond the burnt-out chapel. The photograph gives a good impression of the congested nature of the back turnings behind Hatton Garden into which the jewellery trade had also infiltrated. Hatton Yard (now Hatton Place) still had properties with original East Anglian-style pantiled roofs, now a rarity in central London. There is also a glimpse of Cross Street (now St Cross Street) and the defunct Three Tuns pub on the Kirby Street corner. The skyline is of the City of London, where familiar landmarks had yet to be obscured by post-war high-rise blocks. St Paul's Cathedral, the Central Criminal Courts (the Old Bailey) and St Andrew's church, Holborn Viaduct, can be spotted.

Leather Lane by Beauchamp Street, 21 February 1941. Leather Lane is best known for its traditional street market but it is also an exceedingly historic thoroughfare, its name having originated around 1233 as Le Vrunelane, which evolved into Leveroune Lane, Lither Lane and, by 1682, Leather Lane. In its earliest days, the lane ran along the western boundary of the Bishop of Ely's garden. In the nineteenth century Leather Lane was part of a slummy quarter of London and was plagued by thieves and beggars. There were already market stalls selling food and second hand clothing to local people at this time. The popularity of the market increased through the twentieth century, but the photograph depicts a desperate time for the market traders amid the rubble of the Blitz during the Second World War. The pile of debris behind the car marked a tragic incident some weeks earlier when a high explosive bomb killed one person and injured eleven others. The masked headlights of the car are a reminder of the 'blackout', when minimal lighting was allowed as a safety measure against observation from enemy aircraft. Today, the market is flourishing and vibrant once more and is highly popular with local residents and workers alike. (Camden Local Studies and Archives Centre)

Daniell's Dairy, White Hart Yard, Brooke Street, c. 1904. These picturesque premises were formerly part of the White Hart Inn, Brookes Market, one of London's once familiar galleried coaching inns, all of which have now gone (other than a small preserved fragment of the George in Southwark). During its working life, the courtyard seen here would have been busy with coaches disgorging their passengers and luggage. While it was still an inn, the White Hart played a small role in a bizarre episode of English history. In 1819, Arthur Thistlewood, a one-time army officer, and others conspired to murder the entire Cabinet and seize control of the Mansion House, Tower of London and Bank of England, among other institutions. Thistlewood planned to establish himself as 'President of the English Republic' as the culmination of his operations. In an early planning stage of the plot, Thistlewood established a headquarters in a room at the White Hart and held meetings there and at nearby Fox Court with his fellow conspirators. During this time, the White Hart's landlord was questioned by the authorities about 'radical meetings' alleged to have taken place on the premises. On the day of the planned attack on the Cabinet, the conspirators assembled at a loft in Cato Street, Marylebone, from where the plan was to be put into operation. Unfortunately for them, betrayal by a gang member led to capture and arrest and the Cato Street Conspirators, as they became known, were subsequently found guilty of treason and hanged at Newgate Gaol on 1 May 1819. Following the closure of the White Hart in the 1840s, the premises were used for a variety of purposes and were eventually taken over by the Daniell family, cow keepers and milk contractors, who had established their business under W.H. Daniell in the 1790s. The cows would have been housed in the inn's former stables. The photograph shows a line-up of milkmen ready for the daily round. There were no milk bottles here – clients would bring their own jug to be filled from the churn as it made its way round the local streets on the handcart. In 1900 the licensed cow keeper was Mrs June Daniell and in 1907 the dairy was under the management of Messrs Daniell and Daly; in 1908 this old family business closed. No trace remains of White Hart Yard today.

Holborn tram terminus, Gray's Inn Road, *c*. 1920. A terminus for the London Street Tramways Company's horse-drawn tramcars was established here in 1889, providing a useful new service for Victorian commuters travelling into town from the northern suburbs. The terminus was sited close to the City of London's boundary (as were other termini), due to the refusal of City authorities to allow trams to run in the City itself. Electrification of the lines in 1907 gave tram passengers a faster, more comfortable ride, but by the end of 1938 trolleybuses had taken over and were finally allowed to turn the corner into Holborn and operate in the streets of the City of London.

Holborn Town Hall, Clerkenwell Road, by Gray's Inn Road, *c*. 1908. This imposing building housed the municipal offices of Holborn Borough Council and was opened by the Lord Mayor of London on 18 January 1880. It was replaced by a New Town Hall which was built in Broad Street (High Holborn) between 1906 and 1908. An estate agent's board can be seen on the wall of the old Town Hall offering the building's freehold for sale. A modern office block stands here now.

South Square and Hall, Gray's Inn, c. 1924. Gray's Inn is one of London's four Inns of Court, which were originally set up to provide law students with education and lodgings. Gray's Inn's origins were in the fourteenth century but the buildings we see today are mostly seventeenth and eighteenth century in style although, following war damage, many have been rebuilt. This view of South Square may look familiar but it has been entirely reconstructed with the large building facing the camera resited to the left, thus widening the narrow lane leading to Gray's Inn Square (centre) and abolishing the archway across it. The social centre of Gray's Inn is the Hall which was built between 1556 and 1560, and in which possibly the first performance of Shakespeare's *Comedy of Errors* took place in 1594. The Hall succumbed to enemy action in May 1941 but restoration from 1948 has recreated this beautiful building.

South Square, Gray's Inn, c. 1910. Such was the intensity of war damage here that all to emerge from it were the lawn and the statue of Francis Bacon, centre. The plinth of the latter details the great statesman's life at Gray's Inn, from his days as a student in 1576, Dean of Chapel in 1589 and Treasurer from 1608 to 1617 to his appointment as Lord Chancellor in 1618. The chambers on the right was replaced in 1929 by a new library building whose war-damaged ruins were themselves superseded by Sir Edward Maufe's classically styled Holker Library.

The Gatehouse, Lincoln's Inn, c. 1908. Lincoln's Inn is another of the ancient colleges of lawyers which abound in this part of London. It was founded in the fourteenth century, the Gatehouse to Chancery Lane dating from 1518. That date can still be seen on a stone above the archway, together with coats of arms which include those of the Earl of Lincoln and Henry VIII. The Gatehouse was all but destroyed in the Blitz but was reconstructed from 1966 to 1969, retaining the original oak doors. Part of Old Hall (1490) is seen through the entrance. A group of youths, including a paper boy, have gathered, no doubt attracted by the toffee-apple stall on the right.

Old Hall and Chapel, Lincoln's Inn, *c*. 1904. The most ancient of Lincoln's Inn's buildings, Old Hall was built between 1489 and 1492 and still stands, having mercifully survived the bomb which wrecked the neighbouring Gatehouse. Restoration in the 1920s revealed the brickwork which was once plastered over, as we see here. The photograph predates the building in 1928 of an archway in matching brick which closed the gap between Old Hall and the Chapel, left. The Chapel was begun in 1620 and features a large undercroft, once a meeting place of the legal fraternity during inclement weather.

Stone Buildings from the Gardens, Lincoln's Inn, *c*. 1920. A contrast with the mainly brick-faced buildings of Lincoln's Inn was provided in 1780 when new blocks of chambers, stone-faced and in the Palladian style, were erected to the designs of Sir Robert Taylor. Such is the richness of the architecture within Lincoln's Inn that even the gardener's shed (centre) is a thing of beauty. This extraordinary little building has miniature stepped gables, a Gothic doorway and ornate roof tiles, all to the design of the illustrious Sir George Gilbert Scott, designer of, among other things, St Pancras station's Midland Grand Hotel and the Albert Memorial.

New Hall and Gateway, from Lincoln's Inn Fields, *c.* 1912. New Hall was designed by Philip Hardwick and dates from 1843, its neo-Tudor architecture making a fine sight from the street and a truly magnificent spectacle when viewed from the Gardens with their towering plane trees.

Newman's Row from Lincoln's Inn Fields, *c.* 1922. The earliest stage in the creation of the grand square of Lincoln's Inn Fields began in the 1630s when the first of its houses were built on the former meadows adjoining Lincoln's Inn. The succeeding centuries brought more notable houses and the replacement of others to create what is now a splendid architectural panorama. One of Britain's most revered architects, Sir John Soane, found Lincoln's Inn Fields a most agreeable place to live – his former home, now a museum, is off-camera to the left. The corner house seen here was plain when compared with others nearby, but together with the gloomy shops that adjoined it in Newman's Row, it would shortly be demolished and replaced in 1924 by a fine building for the Royal Institute of Chartered Surveyors, the design of which won the 1924 London Architectural Medal. The impressively castellated Lincoln's Inn Heraldic Office and neighbouring properties in Great Turnstile, a narrow passage to High Holborn, have been replaced by the 1960s drabness of Chichester House.

Gas explosion in May's Yard, Eagle Street, 31 July 1906. Tragedy struck in this tiny close of dwelling-houses and stables behind Red Lion Square when a violent explosion, following repairs to a gas main, killed one person and injured five others. The properties belonged to Messrs May, carmen and contractors, three of whose horses stabled beneath the houses also succumbed. The effects of explosions like this are sometimes freakish – at the top of the photograph can be seen a dresser with nine plates, undisturbed in a room that had almost ceased to exist.

St John's church and Fisher Street from Red Lion Square, April 1941. The air raids of the Blitz were particularly destructive in parts of Holborn and among the casualties was the church of St John the Evangelist (1878) on the Fisher Street corner. Red Lion Square was formerly a quiet backwater of seventeenth-century origin. One of its surviving older houses merits a triple 'blue plaque', having accommodated three illustrious residents: Dante Gabriel Rossetti in 1851 and William Morris with Edward Burne-Jones from 1856 to 1859. The creation in the 1960s of a new road, Procter Street, destroyed what was left of the buildings seen on the left.

Red Lion Square, April 1941: clearing up after the wartime incident which wrecked St John's church, left. Although the church, a fine Victorian Gothic building by J. Pearson, was ruined, the underground air-raid shelter beneath the adjoining Clergy House appears undamaged. The narrow street in the background was Drake Street, which was considerably widened as part of the Procter Street road scheme.

Fisher Street from Red Lion Square, April 1941. A fire-fighting appliance is in attendance beside the ruins of St John's church which had been undergoing repairs at the time of the incident which destroyed it.

Fisher Street from Red Lion Square, April 1941. The brick-built houses and shops of Fisher Street stood no chance against a high explosive bomb but the more massive buildings in Southampton Row, background, were better able to withstand the blast. Fisher Street was once lined by shops but all that can be recognized here is the tobacconist's on the right. Holborn College of Law, Languages & Commerce arose here in 1960.

Red Lion Square, November 1952. Post-war rebuilding is under way, with the framework of the Culver House and Brampton blocks of flats being erected for the Metropolitan Borough of Holborn. Some of the properties in Red Lion Street, in the background, were still in a ruinous state in 1952.

Two
Kingsway and Aldwych

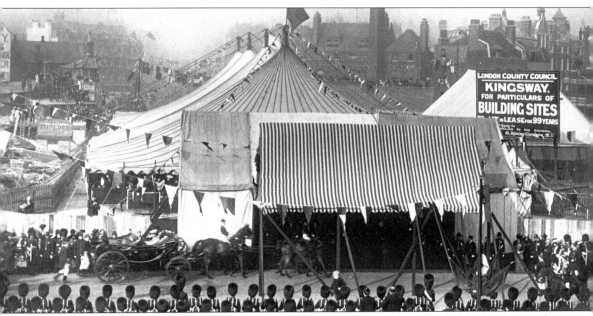

The opening ceremony of Kingsway, seen from Aldwych, 18 October 1905. With the levels of London's road traffic increasing rapidly towards the end of the nineteenth century, it became apparent that a new road was urgently needed to relieve the appalling traffic congestion in the north/south roads in the Holborn area. The existing routes, Chancery Lane and Drury Lane, were both narrow and tortuous and a Victorian gridlock was apt to occur. A grand new avenue linking the Strand with High Holborn was conceived during the reign of Victoria and was to have been called Queensway in her honour, but following the death of the Queen and the commencement of the Edwardian era, a new name, Kingsway, was hastily adopted. Construction of the new road cut a ruthless swathe through the foetid slums of Clare Market when numerous old streets were swept away and others like Sardinia Street were relocated. At its southern, Westminster, end the road split into the two arms of the great crescent of Aldwych but in doing so brought about the removal of the ancient, picturesque but dilapidated Wych Street/Holywell Street neighbourhood with its old bookshops and theatres. The grand opening ceremony of this, the London County Council's first major road scheme of the twentieth century, took place on 18 October 1905 when King Edward and Queen Alexandra opened a set of temporary gates with a golden key. The photograph shows the arrival of Their Majesties at a vast bunting-draped marquee which straddled Kingsway. To the right, a board advertises building sites along Kingsway. However, as this was still a far from fashionable part of town, the sites sold slowly and there was much squalor to be seen through the gaps in the fine new stone-faced buildings. A sight of the Salvation Army's shelter for homeless men, left, is a reminder of this once deprived area.

Holywell Street and Wych Street, *c.* 1895. Another casualty of the Kingsway/Aldwych scheme, Wych Street, right, was an easterly continuation of Drury Lane and ran almost to the churchyard of St Clement Danes, from where this photograph was taken. Wych Street contained, for London, a remarkable number of ancient timber-framed houses, but by the end of the nineteenth century, their ruinous state heralded the clearance of the area to make way for the new roads. The Rising Sun pub, centre, overhung the already narrow Wych Street but, as we see here, there was a touch of modernity on the St Clement's side of the inn with one of the latest electric advertisements, which would have shone brightly in these gas-lit streets. A passage beside Carr's Wine House, right, led to Dane's Inn, which, with neighbouring New Inn and Clement's Inn, was a former legal inn, where solicitors and others still occupied the old chambers. Holywell Street, left, was styled 'Booksellers' Row' due to the proliferation of bookshops, some, apparently, of notorious repute. Anyone standing at this viewpoint today would see the grandiose Australia House (1912-18) with Aldwych curving away to the right but with nothing at all to remind us of the fascinating and populous neighbourhood which once flourished here.

Opposite: Clare Market/Old Drury Lane, *c.* 1890. The construction of Kingsway and Aldwych brought about the clearance of a large conglomeration of overcrowded and run-down property which extended from near Lincoln's Inns Fields westward to Drury Lane. The view typified the nature of the place with stalls and tables upon which discarded household bric-à-brac was on offer. The shops were traditionally tenanted by butchers and greengrocers, but J. Brown, whose shop is seen here, was obviously a dealer in old pictures. Upstairs, a fly-poster with a head for heights had covered the walls but incongruously among the posters was a royal coat of arms. Local tradition had it that this may have been the site of a house in which Charles II had assignations with local beauty Nell Gwynne. The problems of drying large items of laundry in these overcrowded tenements is demonstrated by a resident on the top floor.

The last of the Olympic Theatre, c. 1904. Theatrical casualties of the Kingsway/Aldwych scheme included the Globe Theatre and the Opera Comique, which stood together behind Wych Street, and the Olympic which would have been found between Drury Lane and the now defunct Newcastle Street. The Olympic opened in 1806 but was rebuilt several times before closure on 18 November 1899. The building survived a little longer and was used for evangelistic services organised by the St Giles Christian Mission.

The Waldorf Theatre, Aldwych, 1905. The Waldorf Theatre opened on 22 May 1905 and its twin, the Aldwych, on 23 December in the same year. The two theatres would soon be linked in the Aldwych crescent by the Waldorf Hotel, whose construction site is seen on the right. In later years, the Waldorf Theatre would be renamed the Strand, the Whitney and again the Strand – we see it here as building work was being completed and with a temporary name board above its entrance. For nearly forty years, Ivor Novello lived (and, in 1951, died) in a flat on the Waldorf Theatre's top floor.

Queue for soup at the Salvation Army's food and shelter depot, Stanhope Street, *c.* 1903. A cold night in this deprived quarter of London would produce such a demand for warmth and sustenance for the homeless that the queue would stretch back from the soup kitchen in Stanhope Street to Wych Street, a block away. Stanhope Street was another of the roads which were swept away by the construction of Kingsway.

Aldwych, *c.* 1909. The clearance of Wych Street, Holywell Street and Newcastle Street has opened up a new, if temporary, view of the church of St Mary-le-Strand, left; but amid the desolation, one establishment continues in business: Matcham's Hotel, centre. The end was near, however, for this family and commercial hotel which stood in Newcastle Street by the Wych Street corner. The grand stone-fronted Waldorf Hotel and its flanking theatres were a foretaste of the handsome new quarter of London to arise here.

Portsmouth Street, *c*. 1900. Most of London's visitors, especially those with a penchant for the works of Charles Dickens, make the pilgrimage to the seventeenth-century Old Curiosity Shop, despite the fact that any direct links with the great novelist are highly unlikely. Portsmouth Street had a Dickensian look about it in 1900 with its cobblestones and Poole's waste paper stores occupying the Old Curiosity Shop. On the left, some very modest property accommodated Mrs Christina Wood's newspaper shop and, further along, George Tighe's deed box manufactory. The latter were swept away with the Kingsway improvements when a new Sardinia Street was built to link Kingsway with Lincoln's Inn Fields.

Aldwych and Kingsway, *c*. 1917. Temporary buildings and huts make up much of Aldwych but Australia House had arrived, right, together with the London Opera House, to the left. Bush House would from 1925 replace the huts on the commanding site facing Kingsway.

Kingsway from Aldwych, *c.* 1905. Londoners could at last make use of their spacious new street, the width of which was most impressive. The fine new commercial buildings had yet to arrive, however, and the unlovely area through which Kingsway was built was revealed on both sides. The Salvation Army's shelter is seen again on the left, and further along is a large block in Sardinia Street which, unlike today, ran off the western side of Kingsway. Tenement blocks on the right had had their ends shorn off to accommodate the new road. The London Opera House, later the Stoll Theatre, would open here in 1911.

Kingsway from Keeley Street, *c.* 1908. The first of the new business houses of Kingsway were arriving but there were still many empty sites including one on the left where Kodak House, the headquarters of the renowned photographic company, would be built in 1911.

A new motor bus at Aldwych, by Kingsway, *c.* 1908. A smart, new blue and cream liveried Leyland bus operated by the Walworth-based Central London Omnibus Company has attracted much interest as it pauses by the still unbuilt-on Aldwych/Kingsway corner. The tall block in the background in Blackmoor Street (now Kean Street) still exists and in 1908 was home to J.H. Boobyer's ironmongery business. Part of the Aldwych Theatre is on the left. (Courtesy of David Brewster)

Kingsway by Parker Street, *c.* 1908. By this time, London's public transport was making good use of the new road with horse and motor bus routes and, beneath it, the London County Council's unique underground tramway which was reached through entrances in the middle of the street. A board on the right marks the building site of the church of St Anselm and St Cecilia, which would open in 1909.

Kingsway looking north, *c.* 1920. The 77 bus is passing the church of St Anselm and St Cecilia which was built in 1909 to replace the seventeenth-century Sardinian Chapel in Lincoln's Inn Fields. The church is seen here with its original façade before reconstruction in the early 1950s. Left of the church was a last remnant of the former Little Queen Street, whose line was followed when this part of Kingsway was built. Africa House would be built here in 1921.

Kingsway, *c.* 1928. To the left, the former London Opera House was built for Oscar Hammerstein in 1911 but was doomed to failure, reopening the following year for variety shows. Having been acquired by impresario Oswald Stoll, it became the Stoll Picture Theatre and lasted until 1957. A replacement office block featured a new theatre, the Royalty, now the Peacock. The massive American-designed Bush House is seen in an unfinished state at the end of Kingsway. It was built between 1925 and 1935 and from 1940 accommodated the BBC's World Service. (© Judges Postcards, Hastings)

Kingsway from High Holborn, *c.* 1914. The photographer managed to picture the full length of Kingsway from High Holborn to Aldwych, where Bush House had yet to put in an appearance. The London Opera House (the Stoll Picture Theatre) was in place, as was St Anselm's church, but there were still some empty sites. Entrances to the underground tramway are seen in the middle of the road, together with a cab rank. Holborn Underground station is on the left and a small traffic jam is testimony to the popularity of the new road.

A Suffragette in Kingsway, August 1913. In the early years of the twentieth century, the ladies of the Women's Social and Political Union – the Suffragettes – mounted a vigorous campaign for female voting rights. In 1912 the Suffragettes opened their new official headquarters at Lincoln's Inn House, Kingsway, and launched a militant weekly newspaper, *The Suffragette,* under the editorship of Christabel, one of the inspirational Pankhurst sisters. Here, the latest edition of *The Suffragette* is ready for distribution from Lincoln's Inn.

Lady pavement artist, Kingsway, *c.* 1913. Pavement artists are a traditional part of the London scene but female ones are something of a rarity. These onlookers admire the considerable skill of this smartly turned-out lady as she beautifies the paving slabs of Kingsway with her chalk drawings. As ever, there would have been a hat for the traditional coin.

Kingsway looking north, *c.* 1928. Night falls on Kingsway, the last of the Stoll's cinema-goers have long gone home and the business houses are deserted. This is an atmospheric scene typical of many preserved by the camera of Fred Judge who reproduced many of them as a popular series of postcards. (© Judges Postcards, Hastings)

Kingsway looking south, *c.* 1928. With a foggy atmosphere and street lights reflecting off a damp road surfaced with wooden paving blocks, this view captures the spirit of London in the small hours, although the sender of the postcard writes that he had never seen Kingsway as quiet as this. (© Judges Postcards, Hastings)

Kingsway tram subway, *c.* 1908. This was the only underground tramway in London, running from the Victoria Embankment and emerging via a steep ramp into Southampton Row. The line partly opened on 24 February 1906 and was fully operational by 10 April 1908. In later years, the tunnels were enlarged to allow the passage of double-deck tramcars. Passengers at the subterranean Aldwych and Holborn stations waited on island platforms until thunderous sounds echoing along the tunnels heralded the approach of their tram.

Kingsway tram subway, Southampton Row, *c.* 1908. There was a 1 in 10 gradient into the subway, the suddenness of which frequently caused passengers to slide into one another on the tram's slippery longitudinal seats. Although the subway was closed on the night of 5/6 April 1952, the steep ramp and its tram lines can still be seen. Part of the tunnel was opened for road traffic as the Strand Underpass on 21 January 1964. The Central School of Design, left, was nearing completion at the time of this picture.

Kingsway tram subway, Southampton Row, *c*. 1906. An earlier view of the subway with one tram heading for the ramp from Theobald's Road while another tackles the climb out. The narrow part of Southampton Row was a considerable obstacle to the increased traffic generated by the new Kingsway, but the road was widened when the massive Victoria House was built in 1928 replacing the Albion Hotel, centre, and its neighbours. The site on the left was awaiting the opulent Edwardian development of Sicilian Avenue and Avenue Chambers, which would be finished by 1910.

Sicilian Avenue, Southampton Row, *c*. 1920. This exquisite little precinct with its colonnaded screens at either end is quite unlike anything else in London. We see it here in the 1920s with its bookshops, which remain a delightful feature today. A clean-up has restored the blackened stonework of the view and with its marble paving (reputedly from Sicily) and smart pavement cafés, there is now a continental ambience about the place.

Three
Bloomsbury

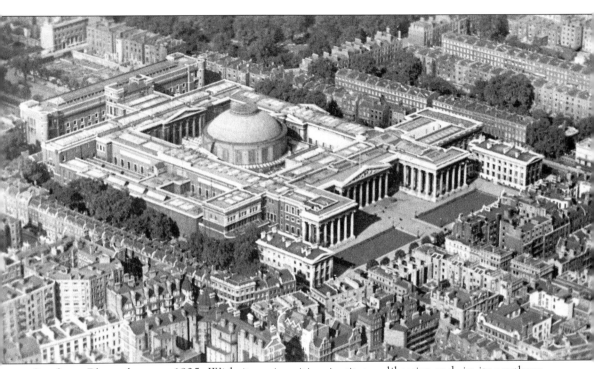

Southern Bloomsbury, *c.* 1925. With its universities, institutes, libraries and, in its southern reaches, the great national treasure-house of the British Museum, Bloomsbury can justly claim to be London's academic heartland. The name 'Bloomsbury' derives from William Blemond, a thirteenth-century landowner whose 'bury' or fortified manor was near what is now Bloomsbury Square. However, it was the Earls and Dukes of Bedford who gave much of the area its present shape by developing their formerly rural estates from the eighteenth century. Bloomsbury's spacious streets and squares, and their proximity to the Cities of London and Westminster, have attracted generations of talented writers, artists and intellectuals, including in the early twentieth century the 'Bloomsbury Group' – Leonard and Virginia Woolf with their artistic and literary friends. The vastness of the British Museum with its great colonnaded façade and domed Reading Room is revealed by the photograph but Bloomsbury's great landmark building of the 1930s, the University of London's Senate House, had yet to be built. The trees of Russell Square are seen at the top of the photograph, together with the long terraces of Bedford Place and Montague Street. The densely packed streets between the British Museum and New Oxford Street are at the bottom of the picture.

Tottenham Court Road from St Giles Circus and Oxford Street, *c.* 1908. Tottenham Court Road was the former boundary between the Metropolitan Boroughs of Marylebone, Holborn and St Pancras and the districts of Fitzrovia and Bloomsbury. The old country road to the manor of Tottenham Court (near the present Warren Street) was built up from the mid-eighteenth century and by 1900 the busy cross-roads with Oxford Street had developed into a major transport interchange. By 1908 the new motor buses were beginning to outnumber their horse-drawn counterparts and there was a new Underground station (right) which briefly bore the name 'Oxford Street'. This was a stop on the new 'Hampstead Tube' (Northern line) and was linked to the older Tottenham Court Road station whose name it took from 9 March 1908.

The Horseshoe Hotel and Meux's Horseshoe Brewery, August 1902. Dismissed by Pevsner as a 'gruesome Victorian abomination' at a time when that style of architecture was deeply unfashionable, the Horseshoe nevertheless still stands. Next door, that most untypical of Bloomsbury's establishments, Meux's Brewery had been decorated for the Coronation, as the nation celebrated the dawn of the Edwardian era. Coloured electric bulbs made up a patriotic message. A long-standing tradition of popular entertainment began here in 1911 with the opening of the Court cinema.

Motor bus, Tottenham Court Road, 1905. The Horseshoe Hotel and Meux's Brewery are the backdrop for a new Milnes-Daimler motor bus which was owned by the London Motor Omnibus Co. Ltd whose fleet name was 'Vanguard'. The bus carries an advertisement for a Tottenham Court Road furniture shop, one of the trades for which the street is still renowned.

News vendor, Tottenham Court Road, 1905. The brewery's walls and railings were a good pitch for this lady news-vendor who finds a moment to catch up on the news. She would be displaced in 1911 by the building of the Court cinema whose amenities included free teas and ices during performances. The Court gave way to the larger Dominion Theatre which since 1929 has shown films and, in later years, put on musical stage shows and live events. The Dominion took a large part of the site of the brewery which then removed to Wandsworth.

Maple's, Tottenham Court Road, by Grafton Street (Grafton Way), *c*. 1903. Today's Tottenham Court Road is famed for its hi-fi and computer shops and for an older tradition of furniture and bedding stores which are a legacy of the early nineteenth century, when cabinet makers began trading here. In 1841, the partnership of James Cook and John Maple founded a modest furniture store which flourished and, from 1851 under the sole ownership of John Maple, expanded into one of the world's great furniture shops. The building seen here, right, is the result of a rebuilding in 1896. Further rebuildings occurred, most latterly in the 1980s, but closure of the store followed.

Tottenham Court Road by Alfred Mews, *c*. 1905. Alongside the great names in furniture retailing in Tottenham Court Road, smaller firms flourished including Avant & Co. on the Alfred Mews corner. As was usual with the smaller shops, part of the stock was exhibited on the pavement but here there seems to be more interest being shown next door where a sunblind shades a windowful of postcards at Henry Hulbert's stationery shop. In a city of double-deck buses, the single-deck horse bus was something of a rarity.

North Crescent, Chenies Street, *c.* 1906. These were the original eighteenth-century houses of North Crescent, one of which once accommodated the celebrated Victorian poet, Algernon Swinburne. Much of the crescent would be demolished within a decade and the London Telephone Services' 'Museum' exchange built here. Minerva House, the headquarters of Minerva Motors, was also built in the crescent. The massive structures now to be seen on North Crescent's forecourt were the street entrances to a series of wartime deep-level shelters.

Bedford Square, *c.* 1905. This is Bloomsbury's most complete Georgian square and one which is still in a wonderful state of preservation, with even the street lamps completely in period. It was built from 1775 to 1780 and boasts a formidable list of aristocratic former residents. The large rustic door cases of Coade stone on all the brick-fronted houses are distinctive features, as are the single stucco-fronted houses at the centre of each terrace.

New Oxford Street from St Giles Circus, c. 1904. New Oxford Street opened in 1847 as a bypass for the notoriously congested High Street, St Giles, bringing with it elegant stuccoed terraces and the shops to extend Oxford Street's celebrated retailing area into Bloomsbury. By Edwardian times some of this district's former squalor had returned, judging by the state of the block on the left which had been smothered in posters. The next corner by Bainbridge Street then accommodated the bookshop of Sol Lazarus, one of the booksellers displaced by the clearance of Holywell Street (p. 39). One of London's first street telephone kiosks can be seen on the right by High Street, St Giles.

New Oxford Street by Shaftesbury Avenue, c. 1906. Some well-patronized horse buses are held up by the policeman on point duty by Shaftesbury Avenue. The hats worn by everyone on the top decks would have needed to be well secured. The triangular junction with Hart Street (Bloomsbury Way) can be seen in the background with the popular Vienna Café and Restaurant on the corner. Opened in 1885, the Vienna specialized in continental pâtisserie in a relaxing environment with newspapers and chess available for clients. The Vienna was demolished in 1939.

New Oxford Street by Shaftesbury Avenue, 1913. So many buses are routed along Oxford Street and New Oxford Street that they create their own traffic jams, especially at intersections like this, where Shaftesbury Avenue and Hart Street (Bloomsbury Way from the 1930s) meet. A street sign, right, points the way along Museum Street to the more peaceful sanctuary of the British Museum, while a toy shop at the far left was a branch of Hamley Bros, who are best known for their grand emporium in Regent Street. At the New Oxford Street store there were sleight-of-hand puzzles and jokes on offer. A branch of the once-familiar Perth Dye Works, the dry cleaners, was on the Shaftesbury Avenue corner.

Mudie's Select Library, New Oxford Street, *c.* 1910. Bookshops and libraries have long been a part of the Bloomsbury scene, with one of the greatest of them being the establishment founded by Charles Mudie in 1840 in what is now Southampton Row. Increasing prosperity created by his lucrative subscription lending library brought Mudie to the newly built New Oxford Street in 1852, where his rapidly increasing stock could be housed in a suitably impressive building, which also ran some distance along Museum Street, right.

Mudie's Select Library, *c.* 1910. Mudie's was a bustle of activity during opening hours with the lending library and bookshop supplemented by a theatre ticket office and a stationer's providing private greetings cards. This out-of-hours view shows a colourful array of children's illustrated books, right, and a gallery to gladden the heart of any bibliophile, with vast shelves of volumes neatly arranged in herringbone fashion.

Clarke & Davies' shop, Museum Street, *c*. 1903. The small, beautifully preserved streets to the south of the British Museum contain a wide variety of specialist and antiquarian shops which perfectly complement the great museum in whose shadow they lie. A typical example was the shop of photographic publishers Clarke & Davies on the Gilbert Street (now Gilbert Place) corner. The shop proudly boasted of its royal patronage and its framed reproductions of Old Master paintings found their way onto many an Edwardian wall. The then new craze of picture postcard collecting was well catered for at the shop.

Museum Super Garage, Hyde Street (West Central Street), *c*. 1925. Private motoring was becoming more popular and affordable in the 1920s and this large establishment was on hand to provide a full range of motoring services, including the supply of 'motor spirit' (petrol).

Bloomsbury Square and Bloomsbury Place from Bedford Place, *c.* 1905. Southampton Square, later renamed Bloomsbury Square, was London's first 'square' and dates from the 1660s when it was laid out to the south of Southampton House, the home of the 4th Earl of Southampton. The house was later renamed Bedford House and was demolished in 1800, part of the forecourt being replaced with the terrace seen here. The building style changes at Bloomsbury Place, centre, where a blue plaque on No. 3 records the former home of physician Sir Hans Sloane, whose collections of manuscripts and antiquities were offered to the nation and formed the nucleus of the British Museum in its earliest days.

The gardener, Bloomsbury Square, *c.* 1905. The central gardens of Bloomsbury Square were laid out around 1800 and just over a century later this gentleman was doing a fine job keeping them trim, although given the size of the lawns, his tiny mower must have made this a laborious task. The gardens are now a much-needed local open space.

The British Museum, Great Russell Street, *c.* 1925. Following the death in 1753 of local physician Sir Hans Sloane, his collection of antiquities was purchased for the nation, together with other notable collections and libraries. These were assembled at Montague House, a grand mansion on the site of the present museum. As more collections were acquired, the need for larger premises to exhibit them became apparent and in 1823 work began on Sir Robert Smirke's monumental Grecian-style British Museum. The view looks through the early Victorian gates into the forecourt and the main entrance to the museum, above which a vast pediment contains a series of sculptures by Sir Richard Westmacott representing the Progress of Civilization. (© Judges Postcards, Hastings)

British Museum station, *c.* 1903. One of London's 'lost' Tube stations, British Museum, on the original section of the Central London Railway (Central line), opened on 30 July 1900 with its street entrance in High Holborn by Bloomsbury Court. The station closed on 24 September 1933 when the newly rebuilt Holborn station took over its duties, but the old street frontage could still be seen until 1989. Note the station's wooden platform; this would be considered an intolerable fire risk today.

The YMCA's Shakespeare Hut in Gower Street, by Keppel Street, *c.* 1917. During the First World War, servicemen on leave or in transit could relax in this range of temporary mock-Tudor recreational huts. Shakespeare's plays were regularly performed here in what the sender of this postcard calls 'a very nice concert hall with a fine little organ in it'. Following the clearance of the site, the London School of Hygiene and Tropical Medicine was built here in 1926.

Senate House, University of London, from Russell Square, *c.* 1938. University buildings dominate large areas of Bloomsbury, one of the most impressive of those built during the twentieth century being Senate House, which was finished in 1937. It was the work of architect Charles Holden whose designs for some of London's Underground stations are held in the highest esteem. Senate House made an impressive sight from Russell Square before Stewart House partly blocked the view from 1985. The telephone kiosk is still here.

Woburn Square, *c.* 1905. This elongated square was built around 1829 and is one of many streets in Bloomsbury to carry a name associated with the landowners, the Russell family, Dukes of Bedford. Woburn is the family seat in Bedfordshire. Woburn Square was to become a victim of the University of London's expansion, everything seen here being replaced by lawns fronting the Institute of Education (1976). The original size of the square may be judged by the fact that the distant Christ Church (built 1831-33, demolished 1974) occupied the centre of this long terrace.

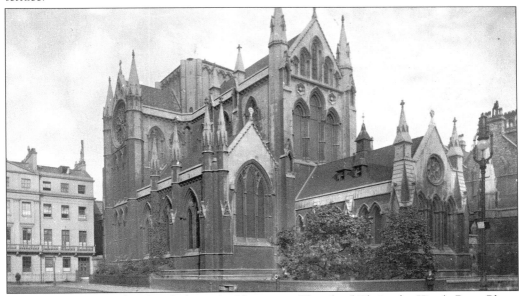

The Catholic Apostolic church (now the University Church of Christ the King), Byng Place, Gordon Square, *c.* 1905. Looking like a miniature cathedral, this opulent Victorian Gothic church would have been grander still if the original building plans had been completed. There would have been an extended nave and the tallest spire to grace the London skyline. The brickwork of the church's unfinished west end contrasts with the Bath stone of the remainder. Building started in 1853.

Gordon Square from Byng Place, *c.* 1905. This short terrace built by Thomas Cubitt around 1825 gave its site in 1958 for another of Charles Holden's creations, the University of London's Warburg Institute. Among a group of rather later houses on Gordon Square's eastern arm, behind the trees on the left, were two in which various members of the Bloomsbury Group once lived, including writer and critic Lytton Strachey.

Hotel Monopol, Tavistock Square, *c.* 1925. A pair of Cubitt houses on the western side of Tavistock Square contained the Hotel Monopol, where there was every comfort for $2\frac{1}{2}$ guineas per week. This side of Tavistock Square is now occupied by the university's Connaught Hall which was built behind the preserved Cubitt façades.

Upper Bedford Place, (Bedford Way), from Tavistock Square, *c.* 1905. Given its central locality, Bloomsbury is one of the areas of London most favoured by visitors for their stay in the capital. In Edwardian days, this long terrace (built around 1820) was filled with boarding houses, but around 1917, nine of them were combined to form the National Hotel, an early stage in the development of one of Europe's largest hotels, the Royal National. Other houses were absorbed into the expanding complex, which together with the Royal Hotel in Woburn Place eventually swallowed up an entire street, Woburn Mews, which ran behind the houses.

Upper Bedford Place (Bedford Way), from Russell Square, *c.* 1908. Nothing remains of these long terraces of boarding houses following the development of the University of London's Institute of Education on the left and the vast Royal National Hotel (formerly the National Hotel) on the right.

Woburn Place, *c.* 1927. Scaffolding cloaks the new Royal Hotel as it rises from the site of its predecessor, the Ardmay Hotel. Ongoing building schemes in association with the National Hotel would eventually create one vast hotel, the Royal National. The old terraces from Bernard Street, right, would soon be replaced by the Russell Court flats.

The Hotel Russell, Russell Square by Guilford Street, 1906. Late Victorian opulence is the order of the day at this grand hotel which was built in 1898 and opened in 1900. This close-up view gives a good idea of the richness of the exterior design with its arcading and wealth of columns around which terracotta putti circle endlessly. The Russell's Virginia Woolf Restaurant perpetuates the memory of the illustrious Bloomsbury resident, who, with other members of the Bloomsbury Group, found the hotel's ambience to her liking and held a number of meetings there.

Russell Square, c. 1922. When the Hotel Russell, left, was built, its eight storeys towered high above the surrounding terraces, but its architect Charles Fitzroy Doll had more delights in store for Russell Square in the shape of the Imperial Hotel, centre. This wildly eccentric building was constructed in two stages between 1905 and 1911 and when seen from the side as in this photograph, the jostle of towers, turrets, spires and a weathervane gave the building the look of a fairytale castle. Sandwiched between these two extravaganzas, the President Hotel on the Guilford Street corner looked particularly sombre.

Guilford Street from Russell Square, c. 1932. The passage of a decade has seen a range of shops built beneath the President Hotel, which by this time was looking rather the worse for wear. This was the heart of Bloomsbury's hotel-land and a sign on view here informs of the 3,000 hotel rooms available from 5s per night in various establishments of the Imperial Hotels Group. The President and Imperial Hotels were both rebuilt in the 1960s but a remnant of the old Imperial can still be seen on the Guilford Street corner where a marble sign set into the pavement still points the way to the Imperial's opulent but long-vanished Turkish baths.

Imperial Hotel, Russell Square, *c.* 1923. Charles Fitzroy Doll's extraordinary design began soberly enough at ground level but having progressed through the statuary, mosaic sundial and exotic fenestration of the upper floors, climaxed spectacularly in a cascade of dormers, one of which, outrageously, was finished in neo-Tudor half timber. Higher still, towers and spires punctuated the skyline while the cockerel on his weathervane contemplated the wonder of it all. The sender of this postcard in 1928 comments that this is a 'topping hotel' and London is indeed the poorer for the loss of it in the 1960s when a modern replacement was provided.

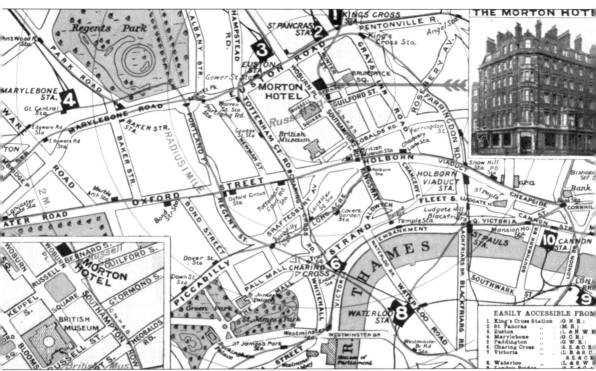

The Morton Hotel, Russell Square, by Bernard Street, c. 1910. Locating this Victorian hotel was made easier for prospective guests by the issue of this useful postcard map. The Morton building may still be seen but it is no longer in use as a hotel.

King's Hotel, Bernard Street, c. 1910. Staff and guests post for the traditional photograph at two of the boarding houses run by Mrs Frank King in Bernard Street. Many of the spacious houses in this part of Bloomsbury were adapted for hotel use in this way.

Southampton Row, c. 1908. This street, once called Upper King Street, was a notorious bottleneck in Edwardian times as extra traffic generated by the newly opened Kingsway struggled to negotiate the narrow carriageway. The development from 1921 of Victoria House, the headquarters of the Liverpool Victoria Friendly Society, gave the opportunity for much-needed road widening. Victoria House took a whole block which included one side of Bloomsbury Square and replaced the old terrace on the left of the view. A gap in the pavement marks the entrance to long-forgotten Redcar Yard with the Red Lion pub beside it.

The Bedford Hotel, Southampton Row, c. 1920. Another of Bloomsbury's popular hotels is seen some three years after a tragedy of the First World War when on 24 September 1917 a bomb dropped by an enemy aircraft exploded opposite the hotel, killing thirteen people. The hotel was soon repaired but has subsequently been rebuilt.

Woburn Place from Coram Street, c. 1905. Nineteenth-century terraces comprising small hotels and boarding houses lined Woburn Place in Edwardian times but in 1937, the residential apartment blocks of Russell Court took their place. The development also included a garage and filling station on the Coram Street corner, left.

Woburn Lodge, Upper Woburn Place, c. 1928. This charming Regency House was built in 1820 and occupied by local architects William and Henry Inwood, designers of the neighbouring St Pancras New Church, far left. The church was built between 1819 and 1822 in a neo-Grecian style given added authenticity by Henry Inwood's visit to Athens in 1819. Woburn Lodge remained a family home for much of its life but in its final years before demolition in 1930, it was occupied by the Carbo-Limo Company, a manufacturer of fertilizers. Central House arose on the site.

Russell Square by Montague Street, *c.* 1905. Russell Square was laid out around 1800 with plain terraced houses on all four sides. Many of these were, as seen here, ornamented with terracotta around 1896.

Delivering the milk in Bloomsbury, *c.* 1910. The milkman in his traditional striped apron is seen carrying one of the covered pails, which was filled from a tap in the churn on the cart. In upper-class districts like Bloomsbury, the milk would be taken in the covered pail to the tradesmen's entrance and from there transferred to household containers. The cart in the photograph belonged to Thomas Pierce's Museum Mansions Dairy, which was based in Bury Street by the British Museum. The sender of this postcard refers to the state of the horse's front legs and comments 'this is a sample of hired London horses'.

Theobald's Road from Vernon Place, *c.* 1939. Theobald's Road is seen just before the outbreak of the war which would transform this scene forever. The Blitz was particularly destructive of property here and in later years road widening would further change the scene. Vanished landmarks include the Hole in the Wall pub on the Old Gloucester Street corner, left, and the White Hart which would be rebuilt on its Boswell Street corner. The distant tram obscures the Bloomsbury Super Cinema which opened as the Victory on 3 September 1921 – it perished during an air raid on 11 May 1941. Part of the former fire station in Vernon Place is on the right, where the Cochrane Theatre now stands.

Theobald's Road from Vernon Place, *c.* 1905. An earlier view from a similar viewpoint shows more of the Victorian fire station, with Parton Street on the right. The twin gables of the White Hart pub are seen again but the further Boswell Street corner (then called Devonshire Street) still had its original buildings, predating the arrival of the Victory (Bloomsbury) Cinema.

Collecting household refuse, Gloucester Street (Old Gloucester Street), *c.* 1906. A Metropolitan Borough of Holborn refuse cart goes on its rounds in this narrow street of eighteenth-century houses, a few of which still stand. Mrs Sarah Garrett's chandler's shop, left, has gone and commercial buildings have proliferated in this war-torn area but the street is still partly residential with Falcon flats further along on the right.

Doughty Street from Guilford Street, *c.* 1906. Doughty Street is rich in literary associations and was home to author and wit Sydney Smith, whose commemorative plaque was already in place in 1906 on his old residence. Charles Dickens rented No. 48 from 1837 to 1839, this being his first marital home. In 1924, the house (seen behind the white-coated street orderly) became a museum dedicated to the life of Dickens. The Edwardian traffic was light enough for two gentlemen to stroll in the middle of the road.

Herbrand Street from Bernard Street, *c.* 1906. Only a few yards from the grand squares of Bloomsbury, but nevertheless worlds apart, Herbrand Street represented a more traditional London of small shops, pubs, workshops and cramped living space on the upper floors. The street lay along the boundaries of the Bedford and Foundling estates and began life as a service street for the more opulent neighbouring properties. It was originally called Little Guilford Street until a renaming in the late 1890s introduced the name Herbrand, after Herbrand Arthur Russell, 11th Duke of Bedford, who in 1900 became the first mayor of the newly formed Borough of Holborn. Herbrand Street's small shops included Jon McCarthy's boot and shoe shop, right, and next door the tobacconist and confectionery shop run by Mrs Mary Osman. Joseph Osman also conducted his trade as a chimney sweep from here – the cart he used to transport his equipment can be seen on the left. There were no proper sun blinds in this modest street but a rudimentary striped cloth did its best to protect the Osman window display. Further along, the Red Lion pub (dated 1894) stood by one of London's lost streets, Bernard Mews, where an enamel sign pointed the way to one of the shoeing forges of James Holmes (the other was in Compton Mews, Brunswick Square). Beyond Bernard Mews were the shops of Mrs Emmeline Dillnutt, chandler, and John Cooke, house decorator. Coram Street is at the end of the terrace. The Forte Posthouse Hotel, built in the 1970s as the Bloomsbury Crest, stands here now.

Herbrand Street from Bernard Street, *c.* 1906. A similar viewpoint to the preceding photograph, but here the photographer has included the National School of Christ Church, Woburn Square, with Christ Church Parish Hall.

Peabody Buildings, Herbrand Street, *c.* 1906. Prior to 1884, the squalid courts of Chapel Place, Marchmont Place, Russell Place and Coram Place took up much of what was then called Little Coram Street. The philanthropy of American banker George Peabody funded the removal of the slums and erection of 'model dwellings for the respectable poor' in their stead. Many of Peabody's model dwellings survive in London and these Bloomsbury examples have been spruced up with decades of soot being removed to reveal the alternating bands of light and dark brickwork to good advantage.

The Hospital for Sick Children, Great Ormond Street, *c.* 1903. Famed worldwide, the first children's hospital in England was founded in 1851, opening in a single house with just ten beds. A further house was acquired and in 1872 a new purpose-built hospital was begun with further additions and rebuildings in the following years to a point where there were around 350 beds available. The hospital's funding received a boost in 1929 through the generosity of Sir James Barrie, who donated the copyright of *Peter Pan*. Queen Square can be seen in the distance with the church of St George the Martyr which was built in 1706.

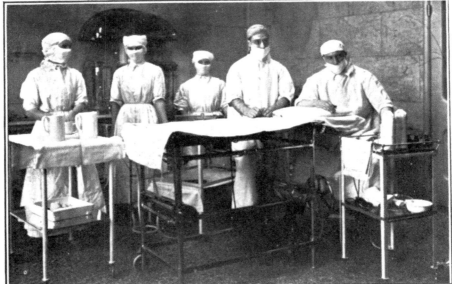

A fund-raising postcard for the hospital with the surgical team awaiting a young patient who has been anaesthetized in an adjacent room. The printed appeal on the other side of the postcard refers to the 2,000 major operations then being carried out in the hospital every year.

The Alexandra Hospital for Poor Children with Hip Disease, Queen Square, *c*. 1905. Diseases of the joints were common among poorly nourished Victorian children and in 1867 this specialist hospital was founded to care for some of them. The hospital was rebuilt in 1899 with wide balconies where the young patients could have the benefit of afternoon sunshine from their beds. The hospital moved away to Swanley in 1920 but the building, now called Alexandra House, still stands and is in use as a department of University College London.

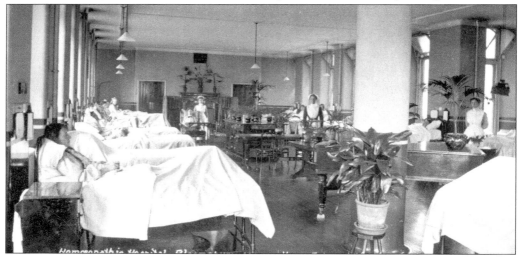

King Edward Ward, The London Homeopathic Hospital, Queen Square, *c*. 1915. Another of the hospitals which abound in this part of Bloomsbury, it was founded in Soho's Golden Square in 1849 and made the move to Bloomsbury in 1859 with the buildings we know today arriving in 1893 and 1909. The hospital's name now has a 'Royal' prefix by command of George VI.

A collapsed house, Great Ormond Street, c. 1910. Great Ormond Street was built up from around 1686 to the early 1700s, and still retains today a number of its beautiful early houses. Their number was diminished when one of them collapsed into an excavation being prepared for a new building next door. The view has allowed us a peep into what remained of the wooden panelled rooms where pictures and hanging clothes gave poignant reminders of those who had lived here. In a room on the top floor (which was in poor decorative order) a row of ornaments still clung to the mantelpiece below the chimney stack.

Brunswick Square, c. 1904. Named after Caroline of Brunswick, wife of the Prince Regent (later George IV), this square was built from 1795 to 1802 with typical Bloomsbury terraced houses on three sides while the Foundling Hospital and its gardens occupied the fourth, eastern side. Brunswick Square's twin, Mecklenburg Square, was built on the opposite side of the Foundling Hospital, almost creating one super-square, had not the hospital separated them. In common with much of Bloomsbury, literary associations are plentiful with another of Virginia and Leonard Woolf's former homes in Mecklenburg Square together with the house in which Dorothy L. Sayers created Lord Peter Wimsey. The Woolfs had also lived in Brunswick Square as did E.M. Forster – his home was on the western side of the square on the left of the photograph. Badly damaged during the Second World War, the same western side of Brunswick Square gave its site for a futuristic residential and shopping 'megastructure' (as Pevsner calls it) known as the Brunswick Centre. This was planned as early as 1959 but after alterations to the design, it was not built until 1968-72, its cantilevered concrete style in dramatic contrast to everything around it. Here also is the Renoir Cinema which opened on 19 January 1972, named after the French film director. The northern arm of Brunswick Square is visible in the background, together with part of Hunter Street. Those houses were demolished before the Second World War; their successor, the University of London's School of Pharmacy, was finished in 1960, having taken thirty years to complete.

Lamb's Conduit Street from Great Ormond Street, *c.* 1930. Originally known as Red Lyon (or Lion) Street, this road's later name derives from William Lambe, who in 1577 was instrumental in reviving an earlier project to supply piped water from a local tributary of the River Fleet to the City of London. Mr Lambe's conduit also provided a wholesome water supply to local people for whom a pump was provided. Before the area was built up around 1690, the rural locality was known as Lamb's Conduit Fields. The view catches Lamb's Conduit Street at the beginning of the 1930s and although most of the buildings seen here have gone, much of the village-like atmosphere remains, more particularly in the section of the street behind the photographer where the old terraces of shops are still standing. The view looks north from Great Ormond Street with, on the left, the corner shop of Ellaman Bros, the newsagents and tobacconists, where still-familiar publications were on sale and Gold Flake cigarettes were 1s for a packet of twenty. The Ellamans also ran a tailoring business from here. The whole row of shops has given way to Great Ormond Street Hospital's Charles West Building. Lamb's Conduit Street post office could be found on the opposite corner, right, sharing premises with Chapman's grocery store, but while this building still stands, the rest of the row has been replaced by Spens House, a post-war residential block. A break in the roof line marks Long Yard where an ancient stone set into the walls of post-war Rokeby House claims Lamb's Conduit to be the property of the City of London. There is an eighteenth-century survivor at the end of the terrace in the shape of the Lamb pub, once a favourite 'local' of members of the Bloomsbury Group. Part of the Foundling Hospital with its grand pediment can be seen in the distance.

The Foundling site, Coram's Fields (the Harmsworth Memorial Playground), *c.* 1930. This large area in Lamb's Conduit Fields was developed in 1742 by Captain Thomas Coram as the Foundling Hospital, a home for abandoned children. Deeply affected by the plight of London's unwanted infants, Coram had set up his first home and refuge for them at a house in Hatton Garden. Following closure of the hospital in 1926, a campaign began to preserve part of the Foundling site as a children's playground. This promotional postcard of the sandpits was part of the fund raising process, the target sum finally being achieved through the generosity of Harold Harmsworth (Lord Rothermere) and numerous others. The Harmsworth Memorial Playground was opened in 1936; no adult may enter it unless accompanied by a child.

Heathcote Street, *c.* 1904. Wartime bombing took a terrible toll of the Georgian houses in this short street, with nothing surviving other than the small building on the left, with a street sign which still points the way to Mecklenburg Square and Caroline Place (Mecklenburg Place from the 1930s). William Goodenough House (1957) takes up part of the street and runs round into Mecklenburg Square.

Caroline Place (Mecklenburg Place) from Guilford Street, *c.* 1914. The residents of these late eighteenth-century houses enjoyed a fine view of the leafy surroundings of the Foundling Hospital, but the late 1930s saw the end of the houses together with the old street name. London House, a hostel for overseas university students, was built here in 1936.

Guilford Street by Millman Street, *c.* 1906. Georgian terraces once ran the length of this long street, where the grander houses were at the Russell Square end while more modest ones ran up to Gray's Inn Road. Many have been replaced, including this block which ran from Millman Street to Doughty Mews (behind the lamp-post), the site being taken by modern flats. With it went the Portland Arms where Albert German was landlord and was presumably supplying good cheer to the driver of the hansom cab seen parked outside. The further houses beyond the wonderfully picturesque Doughty Mews still stand.

The National Scotch Church, Regent Square, *c.* 1905. Grand churches were often built in London's squares but Regent Square had two: the Greek-style St Peter's, whose war-damaged ruins were demolished in 1967, and the Scotch Church, a Presbyterian chapel built in 1828 for the congregation of the old Caledonian Chapel in Cross Street, Hatton Garden (p. 26). The Scotch Church is one of the lost wonders of Bloomsbury, its York Minster-like towers given greater emphasis by the plainness of the adjoining terraces. The church was another war casualty and was replaced in 1965 by Regent Square United Reformed church.

Thanet Street from Leigh Street, c. 1928. The street is still dominated by a long row of red-brick flats built before the First World War by the London Housing Society, but Thanet Street National School (1872) whose tower is seen, centre, was demolished in 1976. Much of the terrace on the right was replaced in 1955 by Medway Court flats, but the further part with, unusually for this area, two-storey Regency houses, still stands. Hastings Street, still with its original houses, is in the distance.

Hastings Street from Judd Street, c. 1906. Hastings Street is seen before the arrival of more London Housing Society flats on the left, and Hamilton House (1913) in place of the terrace on the right. Closer to the camera, the North Trunk telephone exchange took the sites of the nearer houses and Richard Dodd's chemist's shop on the Judd Street corner. The elegant Burton Crescent (Cartwright Gardens) curves away in the distance.

Cromer Street by Judd Street, 21 July 1907. The spectacle of a fire will always attract a crowd of onlookers, especially in a populous area like northern Bloomsbury. Here, a blaze at the Midland Furnishing Co.'s premises in Judd Street (where part of Medway Court now stands) attracted lively interest, especially from the younger element, and there was a considerable police presence to keep everyone safely on the pavement. It was the crowd which had attracted the photographer's interest but his picture has also preserved a fine image of a long-lost local corner, with Judd Street on the left and Cromer Street to the right. The corner shop was in the process of changing hands with the grocery business of William Morris being taken over by Mrs Emma Haley. Edward Haley's fried fish restaurant and supper bar was next door, illumination being provided by a fine gas-lit advertising lamp on an ornate bracket. The Haleys were also in the midst of a visit from the builders whose scaffolding, wooden poles lashed together with rope, was the sort then commonly in use. An adjoining shop was that of John Wilks, corn chandler, while further along was 'Ye Boot' as the still-familiar Boot tavern was then called. The Boot still preserves the Victorian aspect it acquired upon the rebuilding of its earlier incarnation, the Golden Boot, which in the eighteenth century was a popular country pub on the edge of town with a tea room and skittle alley as part of its attractions. At the time of the photograph, the landlord was Edward Speedy, whose family had run the Boot since the eighteenth century and continued to do so into the 1920s. Their family name was perpetuated in a tiny adjoining cul-de-sac, Speedy Place. Although the Boot still looks much as it did in the photograph, the old shops have gone, having been replaced in 1932 by the Tonbridge School Club, a boys' club and mission hall. This is still here and is currently home to the College of Karate. The abundance of Tonbridge and other Kentish place names hereabouts stem from the donation in 1572 of a thirty-acre estate to Tonbridge School by local landowner and founder of the school, Sir Andrew Judd (hence Judd Street). Sir Andrew was a member of the Worshipful Company of Skinners who took over the administration of Tonbridge School and the Bloomsbury estate following his death. Cromer Street's name has no particular significance – the street was formerly called Lucas Street but in Victorian times it had acquired such a notorious reputation that it was felt that a new name might help to restore its image.

Cromer Street, by Tonbridge Street, 21 July 1907. More crowds gather to watch the firefighters as they tackle the fire in Judd Street. Here, the pump's hoses have been attached to the hydrant by Tonbridge Street against a background of Cromer Houses, a Victorian block of model dwellings put up by the East End Dwellings Company. Further along were the original early nineteenth-century terraces which were replaced from the 1930s by the first of the blocks of flats which heralded the almost total rebuilding of Cromer Street.

Judd Street from Leigh Street, 21 July 1907. Another part of the fire-fighting force with their horse-drawn appliances. That on the right was from the London Salvage Corps and this postcard was sent by one of their team: 'This is us at a job'. One of Judd Street's former terraces is in the background with Mary Bormer's beer shop and Nathan Salt's hairdressing salon. Bramber Green, a leafy open space beside the estate of post-war flats, had been created on the sites of the shops.

Judd Street from Hastings Street, *c.* 1905. The plain brick terrace provides a foil for that great Gothic fantasy of the railway age, Sir George Gilbert Scott's Midland Grand Hotel, whose towers and spires have enriched Euston Road since completion in 1874. Judd Street's shops catered for the domestic trade; those on the right would soon be replaced by the London Housing Society's Queen Alexandra Mansions, while the further row beyond Bidborough Street would from 1937 be the location of St Pancras (now Camden) Town Hall, a neo-Palladian structure faced in Portland stone.

Manchester Street (Argyle Street), *c.* 1906. Bloomsbury merges into King's Cross with houses dating from around 1826. Most of these have now gone with residential blocks from the 1950s taking their place. The house on the right by Gray's Inn Road still stands and looks better without the advertisements which once disfigured it. The towers of the New Jerusalem Chapel can be seen with the Argyle Hotel opposite on the Liverpool (now Birkenhead) Street corner.

Liverpool Street (Birkenhead Street) from Derby Street (St Chad's Street), *c*. 1906. This section of Liverpool Street is another of London's lost streets, having been superseded by the post-war King's Cross Estate, which consists of well-separated six-storey blocks. Those called Riverside, Riverfleet, Fleetway and Fleetfield now stand here, their names recalling the local subterranean stream. The estate runs through to Manchester (Argyle) Street, which is visible in the distance.

Liverpool Street (Birkenhead Street), *c*. 1906. The nearer terrace has gone, but the further one running up to King's Cross station is still standing. The pediment of King's Cross Wesleyan Chapel can be seen with, beyond it, a small surviving building which was once a theatre. In a switch of allegiance from one side of the Mersey to the other, Liverpool Street was renamed Birkenhead Street in 1938.

Euston Music Hall, Euston Road, by Tonbridge Street, c. 1907. What is now Euston Road, with Marylebone Road to the west and Pentonville Road and City Road to the east, formed London's first bypass, the 'New Road', which was constructed from 1756 to divert traffic from the city's congested streets. The road was effectively the North Circular of its day and was mostly built through open countryside on what was then London's northern perimeter. As ever, London soon caught up with the new road and the rural views became ever more elusive as terraced houses set behind lengthy front gardens began to line the road. The New Road took its place in London's transport history as the burgeoning railway companies of the Victoria era found it a convenient place beside which to locate their London termini. Euston station arrived in 1837; King's Cross in 1851; St Pancras in 1863; and a latecomer, Marylebone, in 1899. Before that, in the earliest days of railway history, Cornishman Richard Trevithick demonstrated a steam locomotive which in 1808 was the first to draw fare-paying passengers on a railed track – this experiment took place in the fields where University College London now stands, in what is now Gower Street off Euston Road. The New Road became Euston Road in 1857 and from 1863 the world's first underground passenger railway, the Metropolitan, ran through reeking, steam-filled tunnels beneath it. In 1829 the road also saw London's first horse-buses, the well-appointed conveyances of George Shillibeer, en route from Paddington to the Bank of England. Edwardian Euston Road remained leafy of aspect, but as the twentieth century progressed, increasing traffic and road widening lessened the arboreal effect. The Euston Music Hall was a popular attraction among the houses. It was built in 1900 as the Euston Palace of Varieties and became the Regent Theatre early in the 1920s. The theatre became a cinema on 26 December 1932 and continued as such until 1954 when, having been acquired by the Granada Group, it was renamed the Century. In 1956, music hall and variety theatre were briefly revived but in 1958 the building became a cinema once more. The building was renamed the Granada in 1967 but in 1969 the old pleasure palace closed its doors for the last time, having spent its final months as a Bingo hall. Following demolition, the site was taken over for an extension to Camden Town Hall (1977-78), which was built over Tonbridge Street. The photograph shows the Euston in its Edwardian heyday with posters proclaiming the appearance of that favourite of the era, Harry Lauder with his Scottish songs, and the less well-remembered attractions of the Aerial Wrestling Girls. Tonbridge Street is at the right of the picture – the White Hart pub was at the far right.

Four

Clerkenwell

St John's Gate, St John's Square, *c.* 1906. Clerkenwell lies to the north of the City of London and was in medieval times one of its first suburbs. From the twelfth to the sixteenth centuries the area was dominated by its great monastic foundations but when the health-giving properties of its springs and wells became apparent in the seventeenth century, Clerkenwell became a fashionable spa. The name comes from one of these springs, Clerk's Well, which can be seen in Farringdon Lane. As Clerkenwell became increasingly urban of aspect, the spas declined and the area became more notable for its industries allied to the jewellery trade. A decline into Victorian squalor has been followed in recent years by a return of Clerkenwell's long lost fashionable status as a desirable place to live. St John's Gate is the most visible relic of Clerkenwell's monastic past, being the gatehouse of the Priory of the Knights Hospitaller of St John of Jerusalem which was founded around 1140 – the Gatehouse was finished in 1504, forming the southern entrance to the priory. Artist and engraver William Hogarth (1697-1764) lived at the Gatehouse for the first five years of his life and numerous artistic and literary figures of the late eighteenth century visited the Gatehouse during its years as offices of the *Gentleman's Magazine*. Much restored in Victorian times, St John's Gate is now home to the Most Venerable Order of St John who founded the St John Ambulance Brigade in 1877. The Edwardian view shows a typical Clerkenwell mixture of commercial activity around the Gate, with the tall house on the left under occupation by Henry Lamb, masonic jeweller, with Percy Levett, electro-gilders and platers next door. St John's Gate Tavern adjoined the Gate itself.

St John's Square from Clerkenwell Road, *c.* 1918. Commercial activities were encroaching on St John's Gate, with a Midland Railway office and the electroplating plant of W. Canning & Co., a typical Clerkenwell enterprise. The old Coach and Horses pub with its gable and turrets is on the right, with the Wesleyan Methodist Chapel at the extreme right. All have been replaced by bland post-war blocks which do little for the appearance of this historic place.

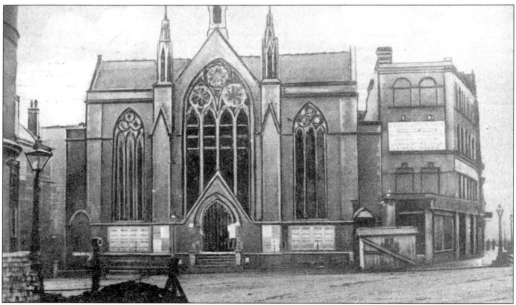

The Wesleyan Methodist Chapel, St John's Square, *c.* 1906. Characterized by its tall Gothic windows, the chapel was built in 1849 and was demolished in 1957 allowing the unlovely Gate House office block to take its place. St John's Square occupies the site of the ancient priory but the construction of Clerkenwell Road in 1879 cut the square into two halves, divorcing the Gatehouse from the priory's other surviving building, St John's Priory Church.

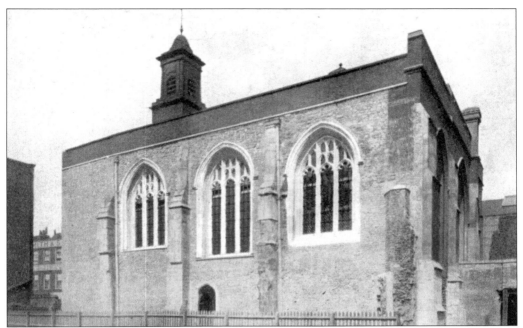

St John's Priory Church, *c.* 1908. Another remnant of St John's Priory with its partly medieval outer walls, the church stands in the northern half of St John's Square but now with a 1950s neo-Georgian frontage acquired following war damage. The twelfth-century crypt has been better able to withstand the vicissitudes of nine centuries and may still be visited. The Order of St John acquired the church in 1932.

The Middlesex Sessions House, Clerkenwell Green, *c.* 1910. An elegant Palladian building in Portland stone, this was formerly the courthouse for the County of Middlesex and dates from 1782. Much of London to the north of the Thames and the west of the river Lea was lost to Middlesex upon the formation of the County of London in 1888, but the building remained in use as a courthouse until 1919. The view is from the bridge over the Metropolitan Railway adjacent to Farringdon Road, which at that time had a small street market.

St James' church from Clerkenwell Green, *c.* 1906. When the great monastic foundations were dissolved under Henry VIII, the villagers of Clerkenwell were allowed to use the chapel of the former Augustinian Nunnery of St Mary as their parish church. When this building deteriorated beyond repair, local architect James Carr drew up plans for a new church on the nunnery site, St James', which opened its doors in 1792. The church stands uphill from the old village centre, Clerkenwell Green, giving added prominence to its tower and spire. The arrangement of buildings seen here is still familiar, with the Crown Tavern on its corner and the old houses running up to the church. On the left, Clerkenwell folk are seen going about their business beside a trio of shops which then included the post office, chemist and tobacconist – there are offices here now. Clerkenwell Green has been a public open space for over 900 years.

Clerkenwell Green, *c.* 1920. The grassy green where children once danced round the maypole and public meetings were held vanished long ago but the trees remain and some old houses have survived. The building on the left arose in 1737 as the Welsh Charity School and following closure in 1772 went on to house a variety of craftsmen and traders, including as seen here, the Twentieth Century Press. It was here that Lenin, architect of the Russian Revolution, worked for some months during his exile in London around 1902, when he edited editions of *Iskra*, the organ of the Russian Social Democratic Party. Restoration had recreated the eighteenth-century frontage and the Marx Memorial Library is now housed here.

May Day at Hugh Myddleton School, Sans Walk, 1919. A group of colourfully dressed children prepare for their maypole dance at this traditional event which recalled the days when such a scene would have been enacted on Clerkenwell's village green. Hugh Myddleton School was opened in 1893 by the Prince of Wales on the site of the Clerkenwell Prisons, some of whose subterranean cells, part of the House of Detention, have survived and may be visited.

The Crippleage, Sekforde Street, c. 1910. This institution was a charity founded in 1866 by the 7th Earl of Shaftesbury and philanthropist John Groom to care for and give work training to disabled girls up to the age of fifteen. The charity operated from a number of houses in Sekforde Street – it was initially known as the Watercress and Flower Girls' Christian Mission. Many of the girls were taught the art of artificial flower making – the group of one-armed girls seen here had acquired considerable dexterity despite their disabilities.

The Crippleage, Sekforde Street, c. 1910. A group of afflicted, blind and crippled girls are seen here, who were taught a variety of skills to prepare them for life outside the training homes. The Crippleage remained in Sekforde Street until the 1930s when it moved to new premises at Edgware. John Groom also founded an orphanage for girls at Clacton-on-Sea.

The Butcher's Arms (now the Betsey Trotwood), Farringdon Road by Farringdon Lane, *c.* 1907. The pub was erected directly above the tracks of the Metropolitan Railway following the building of the extension of the line from Farringdon (Street) station to Moorgate in 1865. The pub is located close to Clerkenwell's far older source of refreshment, the Clerk's Well in Farringdon Lane, to which written reference appears as early as the 1170s. The line-up of locals in an assortment of headgear was probably photographed prior to a charabanc outing.

Field Lane Ragged School and Night Refuge, Vine Street (Vine Hill), *c.* 1907. Poverty was rife in the grim and grimy streets but a number of organizations were on hand to relieve the sufferings of the destitute. Ragged schools were established in the nineteenth century to educate poor children and in Vine Street, off the Italian quarter of Clerkenwell Road, the Field Lane Ragged School also provided a night refuge for homeless men. Their spiritual well-being was also catered for with Ragged Church services, a well-attended example of which is seen here. A tablet in Vine Hill commemorates the Ragged School's foundation in 1841.

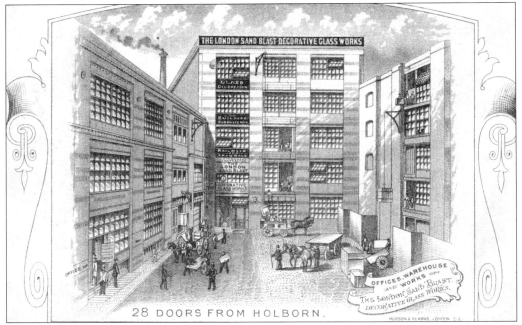

The London Sandblast Decorative Glassworks, Grays Inn Road, *c.* 1900: a further example of local industry. The premises were situated in Queen's Head Court, a byway off Gray's Inn Road near Verulam Street. Queen's Head Court was a final manifestation of an old coaching inn of the eighteenth century, one of several which lay off of the eastern side of Gray's Inn Road. Although the inn had closed many decades earlier, the characteristic shape of Queen's Head Court was a reminder of its existence with a narrow entry from Gray's Inn Road (formerly Gray's Inn Lane) broadening out into the yard of the inn where the coaches would have loaded and unloaded their passengers. The court was equally well suited to its later role with heavy horse-drawn wagons servicing the Victorian glassworks. All traces of Queen's Head Court have now vanished.

Little Bath Street (Eyre Street Hill), *c.* 1900. In the late nineteenth century an influx of Italian immigrants settled in the narrow streets bounded by Clerkenwell Road, Rosebery Avenue and Farringdon Road, creating their own 'Little Italy' with its distinctive shops and customs. The Italians' high street was Little Bath Street and Eyre Street Hill, the name later adopted for the whole street. Chandlers' shops proliferated in 1900 – that on the right by Summers Street sold ice. Although much of Eyre Street has been rebuilt, a number of old Italian businesses survive locally, including Terroni's delicatessen in Clerkenwell Road and Frank Chiappa's the organ builders, who are still to be found at the bottom of Eyre Street Hill after more than a century.

Procession of Our Lady of Mount Carmel, Clerkenwell Road, *c.* 1900. The Feast of Our Lady of Mount Carmel has been celebrated with an annual procession since 1883 when the statue, which is sacred to the Italian community, is carried from St Peter's Italian church through the local streets. It was the first such Catholic procession in Britain since the Reformation.

Coronation procession, Rosebery Avenue, 23 June 1911. Following the death of Edward VII, it was time for the nation to celebrate the coronation of his successor, George V, who, with Queen Mary, was crowned in Westminster Abbey on 22 June 1911. The following day saw Their Majesties embark upon a procession through London's streets – it is seen here emerging from Rosebery Avenue into Clerkenwell Road. The residents of Gray's Inn Buildings in the background had a grandstand view and celebrated with flags and bunting in the traditional manner.

Rosebery Square, Rosebery Avenue, c. 1906. Rosebery Avenue, the first major creation of the newly formed London County Council, was built from 1889 to 1892 and officially opened in 1895 by the LCC's first chairman, Lord Rosebery, after whom the road was appropriately named. Part of the road is elevated in the manner of Holborn Viaduct, crossing the old valley of the Fleet and giving a level run across it to replace the awkward journeys through the steep, narrow streets of old. The view is from the viaduct high above Warner Street and shows Rosebery Square flats which were built in 1890 – the block on the right was restored in 1948 following war damage.

Rosebery Avenue from the viaduct above Warner Street, *c.* 1906. A mixture of commercial and residential properties lined the new road, the former being represented by the premises of Temple Press Ltd, whose delivery van at the kerbside was of the old fashioned horse-drawn sort, despite the name of one of the company's publications. Further along, Barnstaple and Bideford Mansions towered impressively.

The London Spa and Exmouth Street (Exmouth Market), *c.* 1906. The pub's name recalls Clerkenwell's days as a fashionable health resort, when from the late seventeenth century Londoners came to enjoy the rural pleasure gardens and sample the chalybeate waters from the local springs. The London Spa was one of the more popular resorts, offering a variety of revelry and entertainment until 1835 when, with the spas in decline and increasing urbanization locally, it became a pub. Exmouth Street was the main road before Rosebery Avenue was built – the traditional market stalls were permitted once the traffic moved away. The market continues to flourish alongside attractive pavement cafés and trendy shops, its appeal enhanced by the survival of numerous old buildings including the house in which the celebrated clown Joseph Grimaldi lived from 1818 to 1825. Holy Redeemer church can be seen in the distance; it was built from 1887 on the site of Spa Fields chapel.

Tysoe Street, *c.* 1906. Tysoe Street was built in 1819 and bisected by the construction of Rosebery Avenue in 1889 when it was dignified by the building of the London & South Western Bank. This still stands, as does the renamed Three Crowns beerhouse, left. The old terraces in the distance around Myddleton Street, Exmouth Street and Rosoman Street have all gone in favour of post-war flats, while the whole scene is now overlooked by the towering twenty-three storeys of Michael Cliffe House.

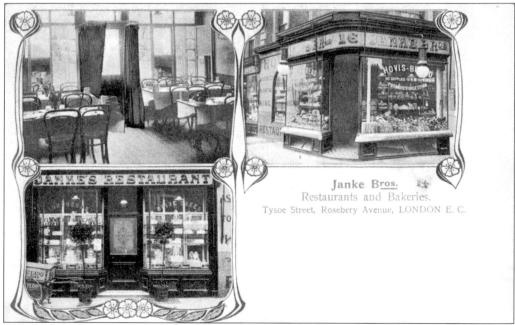

Janke Bros' restaurant and bakery, Tysoe Street, *c.* 1902. Janke's restaurant and bakery on the Rosoman Street corner, was a popular amenity from Victorian times with its cakes and fancy pastries. Bridal cakes were a speciality here – the lower picture shows a window full of some particularly ornate ones. Still-familiar Hovis bread 'as supplied to HM the King' was also available. Janke's handcart was once a familiar sight as it delivered the bread to local houses.

102

Finsbury Town Hall, Rosebury Avenue, *c.* 1907. Finsbury, the second smallest of London County Council's Metropolitan Boroughs, was created in 1900 but its town hall had arrived some five years earlier as Clerkenwell Vestry Hall. It was built in a Flemish Renaissance style to the designs of C. Evans Vaughan, with an extension of 1899 on the site of a former vestry hall.

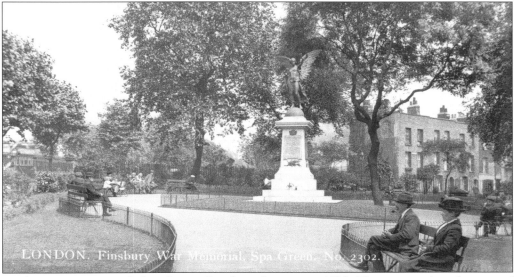

Finsbury War Memorial, Spa Green, Rosebery Avenue, *c.* 1922. The memorial to the men of Finsbury who fell during the First World War was created in 1921 by Thomas Rudge and featured a bronze Angel of Victory. A plaque was added after the Second World War in honour of the fallen of that conflict. This little garden appears little changed but the background houses in Lloyd's Row have been replaced by Wells House, part of the vast Spa Green housing estate which arose from 1946 on the sites of numerous old streets. Many of the building and place names hereabouts are further reminders of the spas which once flourished, including the fashionable Islington Spa, the 'new Tunbridge Wells', which spent its final years housed in a single terraced house in Lloyd's Row, its spring having dried up in the 1890s.

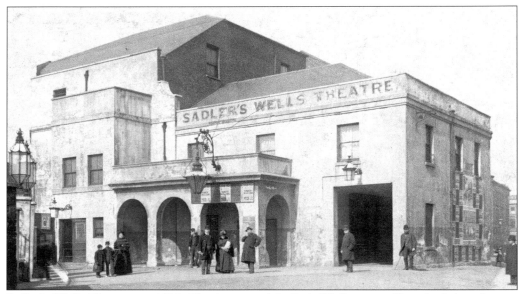

Sadler's Wells Theatre, *c.* 1890. The history of Sadler's Wells, one of London's best-known places of entertainment, began in 1683 when Thomas Sadler introduced a wooden building for musical performances as an added attraction to the health spa he had created some years earlier. Sadler's Wells was rebuilt as a theatre in 1785 and again in 1879 (the building we see here), but its fortunes fluctuated considerably. Sadler's Wells famously saw the first performances by Joseph Grimaldi, the clown, who followed his father onto its boards in 1781 as a child dancer. Shakespeare's plays were performed here from 1844 but by 1877 the building was in use as a skating rink.

Sadler's Wells Theatre, *c.* 1910. Twenty years had elapsed and the theatre had been embellished with fake half-timber, for it was now 'Ye Olde Sadler's Wells Theatre'. This studied quaintness did not save the theatre from the decline which now afflicted it and in 1914 spoken drama was performed for the last time. The building was used as a cinema for a short while but after some years of dereliction, it was demolished around 1927.

Sadler's Wells, *c.* 1936. A smart new Sadler's Wells for ballet, opera and drama opened on 6 January 1931, financed in part by the fundraising of its first manager, Lilian Baylis. A message written by a Sadler's Wells performer on this postcard is evidence of the new theatre's popularity, '…hundreds turned away for *Aida* – terrific reception'. Following the departure of the opera company to the Coliseum, the theatre was again rebuilt as a major dance theatre (1998) but a relic survives from the earliest days beneath the new building: Thomas Sadler's well.

Deacon's Music Hall, Myddleton Place (Rosebery Avenue), *c.* 1888. Early music halls frequently grew out of pubs and the entertainment they offered, with a hall being grafted onto the original building. Deacon's was one of these and on 14 December 1861 James Deacon, landlord of the Sir Hugh Myddleton pub, opened the doors of his new music hall providing more rumbustious entertainment than that provided by Sadler's Wells which stood opposite. The hall was enlarged in 1884 but fell victim to the new Rosebery Avenue which was built across the site. The Sir Hugh Myddleton was built in 1831 on the site of another place of entertainment called the Myddleton's Head, which with its gardens was the resort of the theatrical personalities of the day.

St John Street and the Smithfield Martyr's Memorial church, *c*. 1905. Despite being mentioned as early as 1170 as a highway running from the City of London to 'Yseldon' (Islington), there is little today to remind us of St John Street's antiquity. For centuries it was a road used by drovers en route for Smithfield Market, but by night it was no place for the lone traveller as the road had a fearsome reputation for highway robbery. In the view, the most prominent building is the Smithfield Martyr's Memorial church, St Peter's, built from 1869 to 1871 and demolished in 1956. The row of shops, centre, gave way to the towering Brunswick Close Estate from 1956 but the Victorian George & Dragon pub, right, has survived. Skinner Street is at the far left.

The Angel and St John Street, *c*. 1906. Having climbed the long gradients from the City of London and Holborn, the traveller of old would have welcomed the sight of the Angel Inn at the top of the hill but in Edwardian times the journey was accomplished within minutes on one of the latest electric tramcars. The street scene here is still recognizable, with the terrace on the right still standing, together with the Old Red Lion pub, a hostelry dating from 1415 but rebuilt in 1899. The shops on the left have given way to BT's Angel Centre.

Chadwell Street from St John Street, *c.* 1906. The spacious streets to the west of St John Street were built early in the nineteenth century on land owned by the New River Company, an organization set up to bring fresh piped water from Hertfordshire to the City of London. Work on the scheme began in 1609 under the direction of City goldsmith Hugh Myddelton, whose name lives on in many local places. The houses came later, Chadwell Street being completed around 1828, with the Providence chapel, centre, an earlier arrival in 1823. This became the Zion Baptist chapel and is now the Angel Baptist church. Arlington Street, now Arlington Way, is on the left and Myddleton Square is in the distance.

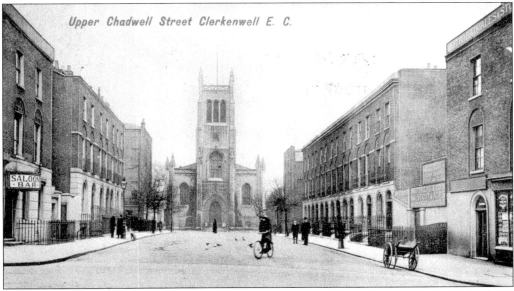

Upper Chadwell Street (Inglebert Street), *c.* 1906. This typically broad street leads to Myddleton Square, where St Mark's church was built from 1828 to the design of W. Chadwell Mylne, surveyor to the New River Company. The street's modern name, Inglebert Street, comes from William Inglebert, the land-drainage engineer who produced the original idea of the New River which was later adopted by Hugh Myddleton.

River Street from Amwell Street, *c.* 1906. Another street on the New River Company's estate, this one dating from 1829. On the Amwell Street corner, left, was Charles Brust's bakery, 'school treats, hotels and restaurants supplied on liberal terms' – a useful local amenity for over thirty years. His shop and delivery cart are also seen in the next view.

Amwell Street from River Street, *c.* 1906. This long broad street runs up the gentle slope from Rosoman Street to Claremont Square which is just visible in the distance. It was named after Amwell in Hertfordshire from where the springs supplying the New River were situated. The house in Amwell Street can still be seen, in which George Cruikshank (1782-1878), the caricaturist and artist who was once styled 'the modern Hogarth', lived.

The Fountain pub, Amwell Street, by Upper Chadwell Street (Inglebert Street), *c*. 1909. The Hodson brothers presided over this typical London corner pub with its marbled frontage topped by some fancy ironwork at first floor level. The whole corner has since been rebuilt with a modern pub. To the left, the original house still stands complete with its wooden shop-front, which in 1909 fronted Mark Simmons' hairdressing salon.

Amwell Street by Upper Baker Street (Lloyd Baker Street), *c*. 1905. The Upper Baker Street corner accommodated a branch of a still familiar High Street name, Robert Dyas Ltd, the ironmonger; the description of the business then was the archaic 'drysalter and colourman'. There was the usual Edwardian cluttered display of stock to which an assistant is adding yet more items to the evident fascination of the group on the pavement. This row of shops and houses was built in 1824 as Thompson's Terrace.

Amwell Street by Great Percy Street, *c.* 1905. The fine nineteenth-century corner shop was that of butcher Alfred Spink, who can be seen standing by his doorway, together with a youth who was probably the butcher's boy. His basket stands by ready to be loaded with orders for delivery to local households. Many of Amwell Street's old houses still stand and several feature beautiful early shop fronts.

Bond Street (Cruickshank Street), *c.* 1920. This street was built in 1845 and named Cruikshank Street in honour of local celebrity George Cruikshank, the artist. The street was later renamed Bond Street but in 1939 it reverted to its original name. The houses on the right are something of a surprise for this area, being of a style frequently seen in London's suburbs, but rarely in such a central location as Clerkenwell; however they still stand and look most attractive. Further back was the ill-fated Holford Square, another war victim for which the Bevin Court flats are a replacement.

Claremont Square, c. 1908. The New River Company created their Upper Pond or reservoir in what is now Claremont Square in 1708, the only houses then being a row called Myddleton Terrace. The main houses in the usual New River Company style appeared between 1821 and 1828, when their residents enjoyed a delightful view of the waters from their front windows. Trees and grass replaced the water from 1852 when the reservoir was covered over. The view is of the eastern side of the square with the prominent St Mark's church making another appearance.

Mylne Street and Myddleton Square, c. 1905. Mylne Street was named after William Chadwell Mylne, engineer and architect to the New River Company. The houses in this short street which connects Claremont Square to Myddleton Square date from 1830. The photographer has captured the charm of this nineteenth-century townscape with only the milkman on his rounds in a covered wagon to disturb the peace.

Lloyd Square, *c.* 1906. Adjacent to the New River Company's lands on Clerkenwell's high ground was the estate of the Lloyd-Baker family who began building on their steeply sloping fields from around 1818. The Lloyd-Bakers employed father and son architects John and William Booth to design the houses, most of which still stand and are of the most distinctive appearance with huge Grecian pediments. The examples seen here are among the earliest and are typical of the Booths' individual style. The houses here run down to Spa Fields New Church, where the road becomes Wharton Street and plunges steeply downhill to King's Cross Road.

Lloyd Street from Great Percy Street, *c.* 1906. More of the Booth houses, but this street is no longer complete with the Cable House flats now taking up the Great Percy Street corner, left. The foundation stone of Cable House was laid in 1948 by Olive Katherine Lloyd-Baker, a descendant of the family which then still owned by the estate. Although the streets were residential, a few commercial enterprises could be found including the builders, William Deighton, whose premises are seen behind a trio of young Edwardian ladies.

Percy Circus, *c*. 1905. Writing in his *History of Clerkenwell*, local resident John William Pinks described the area that would shortly be developed into Percy Circus as it appeared in the 1830s. Pinks recalled the area as Myddleton Gardens, a delightfully rural place where Clerkenwell residents tended their own small plots which were filled with flowers and vegetables. Percy Circus was built in 1842 in five unequal-sized segments around a circular central garden, a most unusual layout for London and one given distinction by the steep hill upon which it is set. Sadly, three sections of Percy Circus were destroyed during the Second World War including everything shown here. The small segment between Great Percy Street and Vernon Street (Vernon Rise) was rebuilt in near replica in 1972 as part of the Royal Scot Hotel. One of these original houses, No. 16, accommodated Lenin and his wife Krupskaya during one of their visits to London in 1905, a stay which may well have been contemporary with this photograph.

Percy Circus, *c*. 1905. This is the largest surviving portion of Percy Circus, running from Great Percy Street to Upper Vernon Street (Prideaux Place), which is seen in the distance.

Spa Fields New Church from Upper Vernon Street (Prideaux Place), *c.* 1906. The original Spa Fields church stood in Exmouth Street (p. 101), having been built in 1770 and demolished in 1886 to make way for Holy Redeemer church. The Spa Fields congregation had by this time moved to their fine new church on the corner of Wharton Street and Upper Vernon Street but this only lasted until the end of the 1930s. Demolition of the church was followed by the building of Archery Fields House whose Grecian pediment blends well with those of the adjoining original houses.

Upper Vernon Street (Prideaux Place) from Wharton Street, *c.* 1906. Upper Vernon Street was built in 1843 to link Percy Circus with Wharton Street – the name Prideaux Place came in 1935. Two of the houses on the left still stand but much of the street is now comprised of Prideaux Court, a series of small blocks of flats. Percy Circus is in the distance.

Great Percy Street from King's Cross Road, *c.* 1907. The sharp drop from Percy Circus leads to King's Cross Road, where in distant centuries the River Fleet flowed through its grassy valley. Clerkenwell Magistrates' Court, right, newly built in 1907, still stands as do the houses beyond, but to the left everything has been replaced by the Royal Scot Hotel (1972).

Cumberland Terrace (Cumberland Gardens) from Great Percy Street, *c.* 1905. This delightful cul-de-sac appears little changed in ninety-five years, with the Percy Arms still on its corner and the houses in a fine state of preservation. The sloping structure in the background was part of Spa Fields New Church where Archery Fields House now stands.

Holford Square, *c*. 1905. The houses date from 1841-44 and again feature Grecian pediments, but are tall town houses this time. Number 30 Holford Square was another of the addresses where Lenin and his wife stayed during one of their London visits – they were here for a year from April 1902 during which time Lenin journeyed to his office in Clerkenwell Green while working on *Iskra* (p. 95). Air raids destroyed Holford Square but in its stead Bevin Court, a complex of 130 flats, was built from 1952 together with Amwell House. This is the southern side of the square with Holford Place in the distance.

Holford Place from Percy Circus, *c*. 1905. This was a short street which joined Percy Circus to Holford Square, whose garden is seen in the distance. Everything here was destroyed by wartime bombing and later redevelopment, with the old street pattern giving way to the bright post-war multi-storey housing of Bevin Court and Holford House.

Granville Square, *c*. 1905. More houses were built between 1841 and 1843 around the earlier St Philip's church (1832). With its plain London town houses and only two small streets and a passageway leading into it, Granville Square has a charm and intimacy often missing from London's grander squares.

St Philip's church, Granville Square, *c*. 1905. Although not large, the church filled the square's centre until demolition in the 1930s made room for the garden we know today. Behind the camera was Granville Place (now Gwynne Place), which led to a flight of steps down the hill towards King's Cross Road. The steps were immortalized by Arnold Bennett in his novel *Riceyman Steps* written in 1923 – Granville Square was the setting of 'Riceyman Square'.

Vernon Street (Vernon Rise) from Percy Circus, *c.* 1905, looking downhill to Vernon Square with its trees and beyond to King's Cross Road where the King's Cross Congregational chapel can be seen. The King's Cross area was once known as Battle Bridge from a crossing over the Fleet but legends of a military conflict here are unproven. All the houses in Vernon Street have now gone and Vernon Square is a shadow of its former self but Vernon Baptist chapel (1843-44) is still there.

Penton Place (Penton Rise), *c.* 1905. What we know as King's Cross Road and Pentonville Road were connected around 1776 by Penton Place – its tall houses still overlooked open fields until the beginning of the nineteenth century. Grimaldi the clown was a notable former resident but the houses have now gone and the massive groups of flats which comprise the Weston Rise Housing Estate (1964-69) stand here in their stead.

King's Cross Metropolitan Railway station and King's Cross Bridge from Gray's Inn Road, c. 1912. The original Metropolitan Railway station at King's Cross lay some distance to the east of the complex interchange of Underground and main lines we know today. The old station was situated between Pentonville Road and Gray's Inn Road and opened for business on 10 January 1863. It was one of the larger stations on the pioneering Metropolitan Railway, the world's first underground passenger railway, which, when first opened, linked Paddington to the City of London at the then terminus in Farringdon Street. This single line was the nucleus from which London's vast Underground grew and at King's Cross further developments soon appeared when in 1868 Great Northern Railway trains began to use an extra pair of tracks, the 'City Widened Lines', for trains en route for Blackfriars and south London. The new services still used the Metropolitan platforms. The original King's Cross surface buildings were removed in 1910 as part of a scheme to build a new section of roadway, King's Cross Bridge, across the tracks from Pentonville Road to Gray's Inn Road. The new road usefully allowed the new electric trams in Caledonian Road, right, to make a straight run into Gray's Inn Road and avoid the series of sharp bends by the main-line station, a hazard which the pre-existing horse trams were more easily able to negotiate. A new station entrance was located on King's Cross Bridge and it is seen here soon after opening in 1912. This lasted until 1940 but although shorn of its canopy, the building can still be seen in a new role as offices for London Underground. Most of the other buildings in the photograph still stand, while below ground, the Underground traveller may spot part of an original but disused Metropolitan platform beside the line to Farringdon. The Metropolitan platforms currently in use date from 1941 and King's Cross St Pancras station (as it has been known since 1933) is additionally served by Hammersmith & City, Circle, Northern, Victoria and Piccadilly lines making it one of the busiest interchanges on the system. The surface transport seen in the photograph represented the height of modernity for 1912, with electric trams and motor buses, which had sent their horse-drawn predecessors into retirement. The motor bus was one of the famous 'B' types, London's first mass-produced motor bus of which there were around 3,000 examples.

Derby Buildings (Derby Lodge), Wicklow Street, c. 1906. The 1860s brought massive disruption to Wicklow Street as the road was bisected by the building of the Metropolitan Railway in its deep cutting. Once the railway opened in 1863, life in Wicklow Street settled down, although its residents then had smoke and steam from the locomotives to contend with. New housing soon arrived in the shape of Derby Buildings which were erected in 1867/68 by the Imperial Industrial Dwellings Company. These blocks have stood the test of time and have had their sooty walls cleaned up and their accommodation modernized. The street is still paved with granite setts.

King's Cross Road by Wicklow Street, *c.* 1906. Writing in the 1920s, novelist Arnold Bennett was far from complimentary of King's Cross Road and its clamouring London County Council trams. In 1906, though, it was all a little more sedate with most of the traffic, including the trams, still being powered by the horse. The shops too, were slanted towards the animal rather than the automobile, with C. Wells' London Corn & Forage Company store on the Wicklow Street corner a typical example. Here, flour was still measured by the archaic quartern, rolled oats were 2d per pound while man's best friend was not forgotten, with Meat Fibrine dog biscuits and Spratt's Patent Dog Cake. Next door, Mrs Sarah Harris dispensed fruit and vegetables, the remainder of the shops catered for the domestic trade and the leonine figure on the roof of the Golden Lion pub was monarch of all he surveyed. All these buildings still stand but there are good street trees now to soften the urban image.

King's Cross Road by Great Percy Street, *c.* 1906. A busy scene by another row of local shops, one of which was King's Cross Road post office. The Royal Scot Hotel (1972) stands here now.

Clerkenwell Magistrates' Court and King's Cross Road police station, *c.* 1906. The Edwardian magistrates' court is seen beyond the Victorian police station which was built from 1869-70. It is now a traffic warden's centre but the former cell block, right, is still in place.

The Golden Lion, King's Cross Road, by Britannia Street, *c.* 1906. Britannia Street, left, was once the principal street of an early suburban housing development which from 1767 arose on Battle Bridge Field. The Golden Lion, which once held a licence for theatrical performances, is still on its corner but the fine beast on the roof has long departed.

King's Cross Road by Wharton Street, *c.* 1907. King's Cross Road follows the winding course of the now subterranean Fleet river but in the eighteenth century this was a most attractive spot with its fast-flowing stream and green hills on either side. It was here that Bagnigge Wells, another of Clerkenwell's spas, flourished from 1759 with beautiful gardens and a variety of entertainments. As London expanded, the stream became polluted and the spa a resort of the unsavoury, closing in 1841 as the environment became grimly urban. A relic of old Bagnigge, a stone from the original house of that name dated 1680, can still be seen on the wall of a house on the right. King's Cross Road was once known as Bagnigge Wells Road.

Mount Pleasant Sorting Office, Farringdon Road, *c.* 1906. Postal activities began at what is now one of the world's largest sorting offices in 1887 when the Post Office acquired the site of the former Cold Bath Fields Prison and began running a night parcels coach. The first Post Office buildings dated from 1889 and through the decades were expanded into the vast complex we know today, handling around 19 million letters a week. The distant turret marks the fortress-like Rowton House, one of the working men's hostels established by Lord Rowton in 1894. The building became the Mount Pleasant Hotel in 1961 and was later rebuilt as the Holiday Inn.

Arrival of the parcel post, Mount Pleasant, *c.* 1902. Wagons full of parcels arrive at Mount Pleasant for sorting and onward dispatch. Much of this traffic has been handled since 1927 by the Post Office Railway, an underground electric line which connects Mount Pleasant with other sorting offices along a $6\frac{1}{2}$ mile route between Paddington and Whitechapel. The line is the private property of the Post Office with the mail trains having the capability of handling up to 30,000 bags of mail in a day.

Mid-nineteenth century houses at the eastern end of Calthorpe Street, *c.* 1906. Phoenix Place is to the left with Mrs Annie Crockett's newsagent's shop which doubled as the Calthorpe Toilet Saloon, a place for the Edwardian gentleman to obtain a shave. The shop is still there (with a different usage), as is the Pakenham Arms on the opposite corner.

Pakenham Street from Cubitt Street, *c.* 1906. These typical nineteenth-century terraced houses still stand but the years have stripped them of some of the architectural features including their stuccoed parapets and pedimented window cases. Phoenix Place is in the distance with a tall smoke stack evidence of the commercial nature of that road. A Clerkenwell speciality, barrel organs, were once made here and there were wood turners and a brass foundry. Part of Mount Pleasant is just visible.

Gray's Inn Road by Frederick Street, *c.* 1906. This ancient highway was once known as Portpoole Lane, Gray's Inn Lane and, with increasing urbanization, Gray's Inn Road. The terrace seen here between Frederick Street and Ampton Street was typical of the road's northern reaches, with a variety of shops including James Smith's chemist's shop on the Frederick Street corner and the ever-present pawnbrokers further along. The central part of this row has been replaced by matching town houses.

Frederick Place (Ampton Place), *c.* 1906. A short street linking Frederick Street, seen in the distance, with Ampton Street. The houses from around 1845 were built by William Cubitt but only those at the Frederick Street end have survived. They were all looking rather dowdy in this Edwardian view – the bright paint of gentrification had yet to pass this way.

A Clerkenwell tram, *c.* 1890. London has had horse-drawn omnibuses since 1829 but their passenger-carrying capacity was limited by the low weight a pair of horses could draw over poorly surfaced roads which alternated between mud and dust according to the weather, with pot-holes present at all times. Tramways with their smooth rails made traction much easier and a pair of horses could draw a larger vehicle and consequently a greater passenger load. Upon reaching the terminus, a tramcar did not even have to be turned round – the horses were merely unhitched and reattached at the other end for the return journey. From the 1870s, the King's Cross area became something of a Mecca for horse trams with the lines of several tram operating companies converging here, usefully connecting with the railway services and bringing commuters into town from what were then outlying areas of London like Highgate. The 1880s saw the tram lines extend southwards, one branch terminating at Clerkenwell Road by Farringdon Road, the other at the City of London boundary in Gray's Inn Road by High Holborn – trams were forbidden in the City itself until the twentieth century and even then they were only allowed in two places. The tram in the photograph was one of a fleet owned by the London Street Tramways Co. and was used on the route from Swain's Lane, Highgate, to Clerkenwell Road via Kentish Town and King's Cross. The tram routes were taken over by the London County Council in 1906 and electrified from 1907 with heavy high-capacity tram cars whose vibrations rattled the chimney pots as they passed by. Life beside the main roads became more peaceful by 1939 when trolleybuses, which moved swiftly and silently, had replaced the trams on many routes. Sadly, the reign of the trolleybus was all too brief and between 1959 and 1961 they were phased out in favour of motor buses.

Great Percy Street and Acton Street, c. 1906. The old valley of the River Fleet may have been filled with houses but the contours of the ancient landscape through which the stream flowed are still apparent and are seen to good advantage in this view. The camera looks down the steep hill from Percy Circus and across the valley floor where King's Cross Road follows the now subterranean river to the gentler slopes on the other side where Acton Street climbs towards distant Gray's Inn Road with its horse-trams and old terraces. The houses on the right have since given way to the Royal Scot Hotel and the elegant stucco-fronted Prince Albert pub was rebuilt in 1922, but Acton Street itself seems remarkably unchanged. Just visible are the brick walls where Acton Street bridges the deep cuttings of the Metropolitan Railway. To the left is Clerkenwell Magistrates' Court, while across the road, John Davis the tailor occupied a prominent corner shop in King's Cross Road.